Sunday Morning
Volume 2

Inspirational Sermon
Guide for Busy Pastors

Dr. Richie Bell, Jr.

iUniverse, Inc.
Bloomington

Sunday Morning Volume 2
Inspirational Sermon Guide for Busy Pastors

iUniverse books may be ordered through booksellers or by contacting:

iUniverse
1663 Liberty Drive
Bloomington, IN 47403
www.iuniverse.com
1-800-Authors (1-800-288-4677)

ISBN: 978-1-4620-5168-7 (sc)
ISBN: 978-1-4620-5169-4 (ebk)

Printed in the United States of America

iUniverse rev. date: 09/27/2011

Table of Contents

Introduction

⎯⎯⎯

Sunday Morning Volume 2, Inspirational Sermon Guide is the best investment you won't regret. It's loaded with phenomenal sermons, and tremendous outlines. This sermon guide is guaranteed to instantly grab the attention of the congregation, enhance your personal biblical knowledge, and increase attendance of the membership.

This guide is not intended to suffice for Pastoral sermon preparation. It's only intended use is to assist when needed to facilitate greater efficiency in sermon preparation. Sermon preparation follows the study and precedes the delivery of the message. Needless to say, the design and writing of the sermon is at the heart of producing and preaching a good sermon. I truly believe that **Sunday Morning Volume 2, Inspirational Sermon Guide** will help you reach that pinnacle. There is no doubt that you will be energized, enlighten, and encouraged with the use of this guide.

Contrary to what some churchgoers may think, Pastors are busy. Pastors do more than teach and preach. Today's busy Pastors are expected to lead their congregations, guide planning efforts, administer church business, visit the sick, provide counseling, and much more. It's understandable that many Pastors search for sermon outlines to help them in their sermon preparation. For those who may object to prepared sermon outlines from an outside resource! Sermon outlines are not full sermons. They are merely tools to help the Pastor in his preparation.

Pastors wanting to use these outlines must flesh them out further through additional Bible study, prayer, and research. Pastors should also feel free to add their own personal stories and observations. They must also add their own conclusion, something appropriate to their personality and congregation.

It is my continued hope that **Sunday Morning Volume 2, Inspirational Sermon Guide** will provide inspiration, provoke new thoughts for sermons, and remind us all of what is eternally important. It is my desire that even the experienced expositor, as he works his way through this guide, will be refreshed and reminded of helpful principles and truths.

Dr. Richie Bell, Jr.
Author

Effective Preaching Tips

I.   *Plan Ahead*—Most pastors can block out at least two full days each month for sermon planning and preparation. Take that time to prayerfully identify topics and/or passages, and then develop outlines accordingly.

II. *Read and Listen to Other Sermons Regularly*—Use drive time or down time to review sermons by other pastors. Include classic sermons. Any pastor can learn from great preachers of the past, such as B.W. Smith, W. Leo Daniels, or Ceasar A.W. Clark, Sr.

III. *Keep Eyes and Ears Open for Illustrations and Quotes*—Busy pastors should always be on the lookout for great stories, quotations and anecdotes. These can be personal or drawn from other sources (such as the news, history books, or television). Keeping a file of ready-to-go, personally collected illustrations and quotes will help immensely when it comes to sermon preparation.

IV. *Select a Passage and Ask the "W" Questions*—Pastors can take any passage (Genesis 1, Psalm 23, I Corinthians 13, etc.), break it down into topical sections, and then ask the "W" questions (who, what, where, when, why) about each section. Going through this exercise will generate plenty of sermon material!

V.   *Capture the Congregation Attention*-Incorporate an attention getting introduction that leads into the message. The introduction can be a story, joke, series of statistics, etc. Just make sure the introduction compliments and leads into the message.

VI. *Explain the need for the Sermon*—Don't let the congregation wonder why such a message is being preached. They need to see right away why this sermon is important.

VII. *Pace Yourself*—Don't rush and take time to explain those biblical passages you choose to read.

VIII. *Dramatization*—Expound and dramatize each sub-point, adding another illustration, quote, story, etc.

IX. *Express Personal Testimonials*—Weave in personal experiences and observations.

X. *Wrap Up*-Close with an appeal that's applicable to your congregation.

Chapter 1

⌐∕∕⌐

God's Alarm Clock

(Romans 13:11-12 KJV)
And that, knowing the time, that now it is high time to
awake out of sleep: for now is our salvation nearer than
when we believed. The night is far spent, the day is at
hand: let us therefore cast off the works of darkness, and
let us put on the armour of light.

There is an invisible war all around us and today there needs to be a modern Paul Revere who tells us to wake up! The enemy is coming, and we need to sound the alarm. The sad thing is many of God's children are sound asleep when they ought to be awake! The church is asleep, snuggled up in her pews with the covers pulled up over her head, and the sanctuary is dark. God's alarm clock is going off warning us to get up and smell the coffee of Christianity. There is no time to push the snooze button any longer!

Too many Christians who have received the Great commission are sleeping on the Job only to wake up and discover spiritually there is work to do but refuse to commit to the harvest by pushing the snooze button of compulsive laziness.

We have too many cardboard Christians, Sutu Saints, and pretending Preachers who are imitators when it comes to evangelism of helping to service the harvesting of souls in the vineyard of unawareness. Furthermore, biblical scriptures reminds us of our obligation when it comes to the ideology of this matter.

"The fruit of the righteous is a tree of life; and he that winneth souls is wise" (Proverbs 11:30). In fact, "The salvation of one soul is worth more than the framing of a Magna Charta of a thousand worlds."

When a million eternities have each lived out their endless ages and have rolled back into the unthinkable past, and time is no more, the soul will still be living a conscious personal reality endowed with perpetual life.

And that, knowing the time, that now it is high time to awake out of sleep: for now is our salvation nearer than when we believed. The night is far spent, the day is at hand: let us therefore cast off the works of darkness, and let us put on the armour of light (Romans 13:11-12).

According to God's clock, it's time to wake up just as the Apostle Paul gave the wake up call to the Saints in Rome in a discussion of eschatology. How much more we need his wake-up call today!

America is in a moral free fall like never before seen in history. The alarm has sounded and we need to heed the call of effective evangelism. But what are people doing? They are rolling over and yawning in the face of God. But Paul says "it is high time to awake" and "the night is far spent."

The devil is equally, if not more, active during seasons of aggressive evangelism. He is not sleeping on his job! Being aware that he has very little time left, he goes all out to somehow spoil the harvesting of souls.

Our days are numbered:
So teach us to number our days, that we may apply our hearts unto wisdom (Psalm 90:12).

I once heard a story about a man who took to heart what it says in (Psalm 90:12). Perhaps you know that psalm; it says that God gives a man seventy years—or, if by reason of strength, perhaps eighty; and it encourages us to "number our days" insomuch that we may gain a heart of wisdom. And so, starting with his current age and calculating how many days he had left, this man filled a jar with marbles—one marble for every remaining day of life, according to (Psalm 90:12). Every day, he took a marble out of the jar—a marble that represented one day spent; and inserted it into another jar.

For years, he faithfully transferred marbles from one jar to the other increasingly emptying one jar, and filling the other. And then, one day, he called his wife up and said, "Honey, let's go out to dinner tonight. This is an important day for me. Today, I have taken the last marble out of the jar." Can you imagine what an impact a daily habit like that would have on the way you live each day of your life?

When you put things into perspective, you and I really only have a short time on this earth—even in the case of what we call a long life. Each day is going by for us; and we will not be able to retrieve it. You could say that we are, each one of us, slowly losing our marbles. And these relatively few years are all that's given to us by God to prepare for an endless eternity. These few years and what we do with them will determine the character of our eternity.

And yet, we're here right now. This day, God has given us the invaluable grace of time to do the work He has given us to do in His service, and to prepare for eternity. What are you and I doing with the time we have while we still have a few of our marbles left?

And as it is appointed unto men once to die, but after this the judgment (Hebrews 9:27).

Jesus said, "*I must work the works of Him that sent me while it is day, for night cometh when no man can work*" (John 9:4).

There are a lot of things you can do while it is day, but I'm going to tell you all the soul-winning that you're ever going to do before night cometh, you're going to do while you are here on this earth. And it may be later in that day of opportunity than you realize. So, how important to you is a person's soul? When one soul is saved angels in heaven rejoices in their celestiral brilliance.

One soul saved is worth more than all the gold in the world. With the U.S. dollar declining ever so rapidly, gold has been increasing in value (now being sold at over $1,200 an ounce). Yet, one soul saved is worth more than all the gold in the world?

If you were given a choice of a pile of gold or the opportunity to preach the Gospel to a million people, which would you choose? Sadly, ninety-nine percent of all believers would choose the gold. In fact, every believer has 86,400 seconds in a day. And no believer has any more or any less, time than anyone else.

What are you doing for God with your 86,400 seconds a day? Do you thank God with even one of those seconds? Do you pray to God for the salvation of lost souls with even one of those seconds? Do you witness to the unsaved with one of those 86,400 seconds? What have you done for God Lately?

God's alarm clock is ticking:

- The **Clock** in general represent the World because it's round!
- The **Big hand** represents God who's the minute hand of time!
- The **Shortest hand** represents Jesus who's the hour hand of time!
- The **Seconds hand** represent the Holy Spirit who's sealing Us until the day of redemption
- The **Battery represents** the life of Jesus that he gave us in order to have life more abundantly.

And it's time to wake up and get to work!

Not only is it time to wake up, but it's time to clean up. In verse 13 it tells us to put off rioting, drunkenness, shamelessness, strife and envy.

It is tragic that so many professed Christians today have the wrong priorities. The average Christian is more interested in their MP3 players and 56" television than they are in purchasing a King James Bible, attending Bible study, Sunday school and Tithing to a soul-winning Church.

It's interesting in (Matthew 6:21) that Jesus taught, *"For where your treasure is, there will your heart be also."* Most people get this backwards, thinking that a person's treasure is where their heart is; but that's not what the scriptures teach. The Bible says that a man's heart will be where his treasure is. This is why Jesus told us in (Matthew 6:20) to "lay up for yourselves treasures in Heaven." By laying up treasures in Heaven, our heart will also be in Heaven.

So many professed Christian's layup treasures here on earth, planning for their retirement and thinking primarily about their own affairs. Jesus condemned this selfish evil way of thinking (Luke 12:21). The heart of such carnally minded believers is set upon their worldly possessions, although they may deny their love of money. Their heart is not set upon Heaven, because they are not concerned about soul-winning to lay up eternal treasures in Heaven.

In the conclusion of this life; tears will flow at the Judgment seat of Christ, when millions of believers have nothing to show for their time on earth. They wasted their life laying up earthly treasures. They enjoyed their old age luxuries and they failed to win souls for Christ.

They never turned anyone to righteousness. They never gave out any Bibles. They cheered others who were on fire for God; but never lifted a finger themselves for God. Scripture teaches that God will reward every believer individually for his own labors:

Now he that planteth and he that watereth are one: and every man shall receive his own reward according to his own labour (1 Corinthians 3:8).

Not only is it time to wake up, but it's time to dress up and put on the Lord Jesus Christ. Put Him on for direction because He is our Lord. Put Him on for deliverance because He is our Savior; put Him on for dominion because He is our King.

So where do you think we stand as a culture, as a church and as an individual Christian? Paul sounded the alarm of salvation in the first century and we need to sound it today as well.

The experience of Salvation happens when a person acknowledges their guilt of sin, coming to God on the basis of being a hell-deserving sinner; believing on Jesus, the Christ, the Son of God, for forgiveness of sins.

"To Him give all the prophets witness, that through His name whosoever believeth in Him shall receive remission of sins" (Acts 10:43).

We are the sinners and Jesus is the savior. We are saved solely by Christ's righteousness and not by any self-righteousness of our own. That's a good thing because we have none to offer God.

All that God the Father requires is for us to come for salvation by way of his Son Jesus, the Christ. *"Jesus saith unto him, I am the way, the truth, and the life: no man cometh unto the Father, but by Me"* (John 14:6).

You've heard the alarm. Now we can roll over and hit the "snooze" button, or we can get up, clean up, dress up, and head to the vineyard of evangelism!

Chapter 2

⌒✺⌒

A Number Heaven Couldn't Count

(Revelations 7:9 KJV)
*After this I beheld , and, lo , a great multitude, which no
man could number , of all nations, and kindreds, and
people, and tongues, stood before the throne, and before the
Lamb, clothed with white robes, and palms in their hands.*

D o you my mind if I ask you a question? Where are you going?
What is your next destination? That's two of the most important
questions for a traveler. And we the living are considered pilgrims
traveling through a barren land. Certainly, death will call each of us and
moves us on to the next destiny.

This earthy house, in which we reside, will one day return back to the
ground; earth to earth, ashes to ashes, and dust to dust. But the soul must
move on to its predestined destiny. Where there's an entrance of the soul
into the body. There's an exit of the soul out of the body to enter into the
presence of the living God. With that being said, "If you live right you'll
die right." Most importantly there's a call after death that each of us must
answer:

*That at the name of Jesus every knee should bow, of things in heaven, and
things in earth, and things under the earth (Philippians 2:10).*

To claim stability in this earthy house is illusion. So those who cannot abide illusion must raise the question. If heaven is not the answer to the question, our whole faith is false, and Jesus was a fool. Matter of fact, have you ever wondered if heaven is truly real? The Apostle John has the answers each of us is seeking for.

There have been many claims of after death experiences; claiming the reality of heaven. There was a story aired on Fox News concerning a boy named Colton Burpo. While in Nebraska this little lad of a boy took seriously ill. As his family prayed at the hospital, it was stated that this three year old kid wouldn't survived; and all of a sudden he survived a life saving surgery.

One day his father was passing the hospital and asked Colton if he would like to go and visit the hospitable people, who helped him recover inside. But! Colton surprisely said, "No, the angels will probably sing to me all day." If that's not enough! Colton stated that he had visited heaven and the city was multicolored bright. The streets were paved with gold, and he sat upon Jesus' lap and played with Him.

If that's not enough! Colton stated that he seen his grandfather who died 30 years before he was born. Strangely, he didn't have his glasses that he seen in an old photo and he looked younger in heaven. Colton looks up at his mother's face and said, "Mom I have two sisters and you could of told me you loss one by miscarriage." But! You see his mom never informed him about his first sister's death, and was amazed at his testimony.

Listen! No one ever explained angels to Colton. No one ever explained heaven to Colton, nor ever introduced him to Jesus. He experienced it for himself.

John in the text informs us on what to expect concerning heaven:

I. John's Surprised Visitation:

John has been abandoned on the Isle of Patmos. After being boiled and escaping a hot pot of oil. He has been left out there to die by the salvaging of wild beast! While on the Isle of Patmos—John was there for one purpose—to receive the revelation of things yet to come.

Jesus our heavenly host felt John's suffering and invited him to heaven. John saw and spoke with Him in his glorious splendor. He is invited to look into the throne room of heaven.

The invitation Jesus offers to John is to come and see what must take place after this. He allows John to preview the book of destiny of what will unfold at the end of time. Out of the book of destiny, John witnesses things which were unspeakable in explanation; but writable by hand with the guidance of the Holy Spirit. Write what you see and hear! This is what Jesus commanded John and present to the seven churches of Asia Minor.

This same invitation given to John is universal and timeless in scope, and available to anyone at anytime. Here's what I'm trying to express: To be "somebody" in Hollywood or a "bigwig" in politics, you must be at all the right parties and functions to be with all the right people. When Prince Charles and Lady Di visited Washington, D.C. and a social gala was given in their honor, the hot topic was, "Who will be invited to the party?" The "have's" get an invitation; and the "have not's" don't. Haven't we all felt the sting of being left out when others were invited and we were treated as misfits? But! Jesus died that each of us might inherit heaven equally.

Heaven in reality is real:

- Jacob saw angel ascending and descending from heaven upon a ladder;
- Elijah was taken into heaven by a whirlwind;

- Enoch walked into heaven because God's house was closer than his own house;
- Jesus saw Satan fall from heaven like lighting;
- Paul even visited heaven on one occasion.

So when it comes to what John saw; Jesus showed and told him the things of heaven and I believe it. So the question is, "Will you miss hell, and make heaven?" Just because you're religious; don't mean you'll make heaven. You can be religious and lost! We shouldn't be working to get to heaven, but believing to make it there.

II. John's Splendid Vision:

There's an elder, who is serving as John's spiritual tour guide, he shows him a gigantic multitude of people. Like some huge victory party, they all stand around the throne of God in heaven, clothed in dazzling white robes and carrying palm branches of victory in their hands. And then the tour guide elder gently nudges John and says, "John you know who these people are, don't you?" John doesn't quite dare to hope. It would be nice, but it just can't be.

John observes a number of 144,000 from the tribes of Israel; but he takes a second snapshot and sees "a great multitude." He witnesses a number that heaven couldn't count. There are millions, maybe even billions and trillions in his sight. He sees a number that is even greater than the number of angels he saw around the throne of God (Revelation 5:11). Amazingly the company of Christians is beyond counting. These are those who have endured the great tribulational period.

It was quite a sight to behold! John saw infants, toddlers, youngsters, teens, young adults, older adults and seasoned senior citizens. John saw those who bore the awful scars of life. They have been through birth defects, accidents, violent crimes, violent deaths and serious surgeries.

They were from a multitude of cultures, different towns and cities and countries, from the seaside to the mountaintops and everywhere in between. Yet they all related to each other, loved and understood each other, and worship with one another because of what they all had in common. When they came down to the end of their rope during the great tribulational period they tied a knot and held on.

Here are overcomers enjoying the comfort of heaven and worshiping God is what they all had in common. They are not like the 21st century church where we jump high in public worship and live low in private wrongness!

These were true worshippers, worshipping God in stereo! Some believe that heaven will be monotone. Some believe that heaven is just an illusion or rather boring. Satan need not convince us that heaven doesn't exist. He needs only to convince us that heaven is a boring unearthly place.

John the Revelator's vision provides a glorious picture of what will be in heaven. There will be a high wall with twelve gates and twelve angels at the gates. The wall will have twelve foundations. The gates will be named for the twelve tribes of Israel and the foundations for the twelve apostles of Jesus Christ.

The city will be foursquare, with walls of jasper. The walls foundations will be adorned with precious gemstones. The gates will be pearls. The city itself will be made of pure gold and the streets will be paved with transparent gold. I'm planning on being with God in heaven to crown Jesus, Lord of lords and Kings of kings.

The way to heaven is through Jesus, God's Word made flesh:

- He died until three worlds shook: Heaven, Earth, and Hell.
- He died until the sun had a hemorrhage and dripped away in blood.
- He died until the soldier said, "He must be the Son of God."
- As our Good Sheppard He died for us.
- As our Great Sheppard He got up for us.
- As of Grand Sheppard He returns for us.

When our Lord redeems this broken world, we will be ushered into the New Jerusalem at last. The new heaven and the new earth will be the dream home come true. Until then, Like John we can see it from a distance. There is only one way to heaven and those who follow that way are guaranteed to get there. But not everyone is following that way. Are you?

Chapter 3

⤬

Stay on the Wall

(Nehemiah 6:14 KJV)
My God, think thou upon Tobiah and Sanballat
according to these their works, and on the prophetess
Noadiah, and the rest of the prophets, that would have
put me in fear.

Nehemiah in the past visited the Palace of Shushan when he encountered a group of men from Jerusalem. Judah has been carried into exile and it had been a long time since Nehemiah had heard anything concerning his homeland. The news was not good. The men had told Nehemiah that the remnant that had survived the exile was in great trouble and shame. The walls were broken down and the gates had been burned. When he heard this news he began to cry and became greatly distressed and depressed. He took the situation to the Lord with prayer and fasting. Thereafter, with a sense of urgency, Nehemiah decided to start a building program.

Here is Nehemiah the cupbearer for king Artaxerxes to assure that he would not drink poison. Here is a prophet supporting the vision of an invisible God. Here is a man who was vigorous and soon will challenge those who were venomous towards the work.

Whenever God calls us to do something often the excitement that initially accomplished it can soon turn into frustration. It's amazing how the amount of opposition, frustration and fatigue we experience often begins as soon as we start to move towards the direction God has given us.

I. Nehemiah's Anointing:

Nehemiah is a great example of staying focused and committed to an important task. This Israelite Nehemiah has gone through the task of living in exile in Babylon. One day the king asked Nehemiah why he seemed so sad.

Nehemiah replied, "Why should not my countenance be sad, when the city, the place of my fathers' grave, lieth waste, and the gates thereof are consumed with fire?"

God gave Nehemiah an anointing. And his anointing was so evident that it rubbed off on the king who showed him favor to inspect and rebuild the walls to the city. In every task God gives us; he will place upon us favor. But! Our enemies think God's favor isn't fair! Remember it's dangerous to touch God's anointed one who's been favored in the Lord.

II. Nehemiah's Assignment:

One thing that clearly emerges from this book is that life is a battle from beginning to end. Nehemiah ran into opposition the moment he set his heart to obey God's command to rebuild the walls and gates of Jerusalem. He faced difficulty before he even got to the city. Then, after he reached Jerusalem enemies rose up to oppose everything he did. You may not yet have experienced all that in your Christian life, but you will! The Apostle Paul warns, "Our struggle is not against flesh and blood," (Ephesians 6:12). Men and women, other humans, are not really our problem.

What we are up against is invisible forces: *"the world powers of darkness"* (Ephesians 6:12b), Paul calls them. These same enemies are found in the book of Nehemiah also. Thus we are confronted by an invisible enemy who hates law and order, and justice and peace. He loves to mangle, trap, destroy and murder. He lives to oppose the work of God in creating harmony, beauty, love and respect for one another. That is what we are battling.

But that didn't stop Nehemiah's assignment! When nighttime would tip toe in, and the sun would rest her head, Nehemiah would ride upon a horse and inspect the walls for rebuilding; and share with the people who became willing working, that God has approved of the reconstruction.

But Satan was waiting and watching through his binoculars of adversity. He was conspiring plans to derail the Lord's work. What a tuff assignment from the Lord Nehemiah would endure.

In fact, in the Bible we find numerous accounts of people to whom God gave various assignments in which He expected them to succeed by taking specific actions that He had commanded them to take. Here's what I'm trying to explain:

- God told Abraham to sacrifice his beloved son Isaac (Genesis 22:2).
- God told Noah to build a giant ark by which he, his extended family, and Earth's animals could be saved from a coming universal flood (Genesis 6:14).
- God told Moses to lead the Israelites out of Egypt (Exodus 3:10).
- God told Joshua to lead the Israelites to battle their enemies as they occupied the Promised Land of Canaan (Joshua 1:1-9).
- God told Jonah to preach to the huge city of Nineveh in order to convince its inhabitants to repent of their sins (Jonah 1:2).
- God told Nehemiah to rebuild the walls and city of Jerusalem (Nehemiah 2:12).
- God told Hosea to marry a harlot in order to show the Israelites that they had polluted their service to God (Hosea 1:2).
- Christ told His disciples to take the Gospel to the entire world (Matthew 28:19-20).

- Christ told Christians to be faithful even unto death (Revelation 2:10).

Do you think it was easy for them? No! It was not easy for those people to carry out such tasks or to endure such suffering. And no catchy sayings or cute mottos could make their lives any easier. So what was it, then, that helped such individuals succeed in carrying out the tough assignments that God had given them? Answer: It was their Faith!

III. Nehemiah's Action:

In the first five chapters of the book of Nehemiah; it tell of the ways Satan tried to stop the people from rebuilding. Satan tried **derision** by laughing at the work, **discouragement** that the project would be a complete failure, **danger** of bodily harm, **discord** to get the people to fight against each other, **depletion** of taking away needed resources to complete the assignment.

In Chapter six, following a series of attacks and threats against him in an effort to intimidate him, the enemies of Nehemiah suddenly change their tactics. Suddenly they resort to **distraction** of friendliness and persuasion.

Listen to what Nehemiah testifies. "*When word came to Sanballat, Tobiah, Geshem the Arab and the rest of our enemies that I had rebuilt the wall and not a gap was left in it—though up to that time I had not set the doors in the gates—Sanballat and Geshem sent me this message: Come, let us meet together in one of the villages on the plain of Ono. But they were scheming to harm me; so I sent messengers to them with this reply: I am carrying on a great project and cannot go down. Why should the work stop while I leave it and go down to you?" Four times they sent me the same message, and each time I gave them the same answer*" (Nehemiah 6:1-4 NIV).

These individuals once enemies; suddenly become Nehemiah's friends and invited him to a conference down on the plain of Ono. But Nehemiah senses danger: "they were scheming to harm me," he says. Some commentators suggest that they were trying to trick him into leaving Jerusalem, where he had armed support, to come to a conference where they could set upon him and perhaps kill him. Nehemiah evidently senses this. He firmly declines, saying, "I am carrying on a great project, and I cannot go down. Why should the work stop while I leave it and go down to you?"

They could not stop the work of building by threat and attack, so they switched their tactics. You will experience this too when you try to correct wrong things in your life. It is possible that your friends will become your most dangerous foes.

Nehemiah was persistent in his refusal. Here is his reason: "I am doing a great work," he says. "I have a great calling. God has committed a tremendous project to me, and if I leave, it will be threatened." One of the most helpful things that we can do to resist temptation is to remember that God has called us to a great task. "*So this wall was finished*" (Nehemiah 6:15).

Chapter 4

⌒*⌒*⌒

My Mission Is Accomplished

(John 19:30 KJV)
When Jesus therefore had received the vinegar, he
said, It is finished: and he bowed his head, and gave
up the ghost.

There are three words in our English language that, when spoken as one, can signify either the sincere joy and satisfaction or the deepest sorrow and misery. These words are: "It is finished." When they are used by graduating seniors or marathon runners finishing out their last term; you know it's a sign of joy and relief. When they are used by a senior who has failed his final exam or by a fireman who has run out of water, or by a Miami Heat fan watching them play the Dallas Mavericks, you know it is a sign of dejection and frustration.

Have you ever felt frustrated; think about it for a moment? I mean really frustrated? Have you ever let a difficult or undesirable circumstance ruin your mood and sour your mind-set toward the day? I imagine each of us has felt some degree of frustration at one time or another. I wouldn't be telling you anything new if I said that frustration, and fatigued is a part of life. But! It comes to a point in your life, that whatever has bugged you, "You just can't take it anymore." You are now ready to dry up your last tears, feel the last pains of betrayal, and toss and turn one more time with your last agony. And now you're ready to testify to the whole world, "My mission is accomplished!"

In the text, Jesus is hanging on the cross, and the Jews are watching him as a theatrical. They were once angered at Jesus. And they were determined that he would not leave their traditionalized religion alone, and therefore had to devise a scheme to get rid of him. So, they persuaded the Roman governor Pilate to have him arrested, find him guilty of breaking the laws of Judaism, and kill him by way of crucifixion. They tried their best to make Jesus give up and throw in the towel of defeat. But! Listen, when the world says, "Give up," Hope whispers, "Keep trying."

The Jews thought in their state of carnality that Jesus was just a mere human and watched him throughout his ministry; while at the same time planned a conspiracy against him. The Jews suffered from a viral case of spiritual malnutrition. They fail to recognize this man who's hanging on the cross as God our Creator, Maker, and Redeemer! They placed obstacles in his way, but Jesus would encourage us that, "If you can find a path with no obstacles, it probably doesn't lead anywhere."

Jesus like us on his human side had human emotions, much the same as compared to our limitations. He preached with compassion, explained the dangers of condemnation, exposed the religious leader's corruptions, shed the tears of concern over Jerusalem, slept in the comfort of another man's home, ate from another man's table, and cured another man's disease and now as God's only Son will be crucified for another man's sins. After all of his preaching and teaching and death; the Jews refused to still follow and listen to him as the Saviour of the world.

Have you ever felt frustrated when people wouldn't listen to you while teaching from the Bible? Have you felt frustrated when they made you the issue as to why they wouldn't listen? Some of them looked down on your age and said, "You're too young or old for them to respect what you said. Who are you to tell them what they should do?" Or they may turn up their nose and say, "You're not from around here, are you?" Or they may think you're inadequate to help them because, "You don't understand their troubles. You haven't gone through what they have experienced."

People have a million excuses why they won't listen to you teach them the authenticity of Salvation. What I say is: keep teaching the word anyway, and when they say things like that and frustrate you because they won't listen, know you are in good company with Jesus.

I. The Redemptive Work of Jesus:

Jesus is hanging on the cross atop of Mount Cavalry. Can you see Him there? Three crosses stood on Mount Calvary the day he died. Three condemned men hung on those crosses, two of which were thieves, each endured the same death sentence; yet each viewed life and death differently as they hung there dying. While each of them hung on a cross, there was jeering from the crowds, the soldiers, and the religious people. They decided to throw a block party! But what the people did not realize was that those thieves represented them. A thief is someone who continually takes from someone else, and that is exactly what a person is without Jesus Christ—a thief from the chief thief himself—Satan. Let's take a glimpse of these three crosses.

One man hung on a **Cross of Rejection**. This man mocked Jesus. I don't know what he knew about the Lord, I only know he repeated what he heard others say as he hung there embittered by his own powerlessness and apparent weakness of the Savior who hung beside him. What is one to make of a Messiah who cannot even save Himself? In other words he saw faults Jesus did not have, and failed to acknowledge his own. He was dying with Jesus beside him but not within him. He had a chance to accept Him, but he blew it! I want to suggest to you, "When it comes to your Salvation, Don't blow it!" This man was dying among the living and decided to stick with the crowd.

Let me hurry and say, "Some crowds you hang out with will send you to hell!" But if you are going through hell right now, because of the crowds that you hang out with, don't stop! Please keep going there's a way out!

The other man hung on a **Cross of Repentance**. This man mocked at first but then admitted his own guilt. He saw in Jesus a power that the first criminal missed. Seeing that power, the second criminal begged for mercy. He could do nothing to amend his past; he could promise nothing in a bargain for the future. Instead he simply asked, "Lord, remember me when You come into Your Kingdom." "Don't remember my sins but remember me Lord."

Finally, in between two thieves hangs one on a **Cross of Redemption**. Jesus suffers there, arms stretched out, reaching wide in love to all who will receive Him. Jesus couldn't take it anymore seeing us headed for a dead end! So, the shedding of His precious blood caused us to make a u-turn.

The cross on which He suffered canceled out any need for despair, no matter what your past is all about! No matter how bleak and hopeless your future looks, from the cross of Christ flows endless power to forgive and to love. The power of the cross reveals the Glory of God's love in Christ.

The thieves deserved to die. We deserve to die. But Jesus did not deserve to die. Jesus being lifted up on the cross between the two thieves represents the fact that He has identified with us. Before we could be lifted up to Jesus' level as kings and priests, He had to be brought down to ours. He laid aside His great position in heaven, humbled Himself, and became obedient unto death, even the death of the cross. Jesus was our Great Substitute on the cross.

II. The Remarkable Mission of Jesus:

Jesus had done everything, endured everything, spoken everything, and suffered long enough. Now it was time to die. When He spoke these words, He took care to tell those who cared to listen that He knew in whose care His soul was to rest. It was like one little final piece of housekeeping, then he died, saying **"Father, into Thy hands I commit My spirit."**

These next-to-last words from the cross, **"It is finished,"** are really only one word in the Greek, ***tetelestai***. There are other words in the bible which tell us about His pain, or tell us something about His great love, or tell us something about the deliberate nature of His death for us. But these words tell us about His great work of redeeming fallen mankind from sin. They tell us that it is complete. **It is finished.** These words, **"It is finished,"** specify not the end of Jesus' life, but the completion of His task.

This means Christ's work of suffering is now complete. Oh! How our Lord suffered. The cup of wrath has been drained. The wages of sin have been paid. The disgrace and shame, the suffering and agony, are past. Never again shall He experience pain. Never again shall He endure the taunts and slaps of those who hated Him. Never again shall He be in the hands of His enemies. Never again shall He be in darkness. Never again will God's presence be taken from Him. "It is finished," was the cry, of the Son of Man who died. He hung in there; not only by the nails but by the hedges of His love for us. He is the way, truth and the life!

This is a comfort for us. When our hour comes, Jesus has shown us the way. He has gone before us through the door of death, and He will bring us each safely though. He knows the way. He is the Way, and the Door—and the Life beyond that Door. We can die, as Jesus died, without fear and without a doubt about where we are going, or to whom. And we can be sure that there is nothing left for us to do, no test at the end, no final moment of challenge, because Jesus did all that we need done, and then told us that the mission was accomplished.

Chapter 5

⌒⁂⌒

The Sweetest Name I Know

(Matthew 1:23 KJV)
*And she shall bring forth a son, and thou shalt call his
name JESUS: for he shall save his people from their sins.*

Ow important are names? What kinds of images are created when we hear names like: Rosa Parks, Nate King Cole, George Washington Carver, Martin Luther King Jr., Harriet Tubman, Jackie Robinson, Sugar Ray Leonard, or Barack Hussein Obama?

Obviously there is great power in names; they reflect a myriad of images and ideas in our minds. They identify certain traits or characteristics when they are names of people, groups or nations because they connect us to the past through our histories.

Here in our text the angel mentions the name of Jesus (Matthew 1:21-23). There is something special about the name Jesus for the angel said, He will save His people from their sins. It is a name given to Him by heaven (Matthew 1:21; Luke 1:31). The name Jesus is a name that has been exalted by God the Father:

"Wherefore God also hath highly exalted him, and given him a name which is above every name: That at the name of Jesus every knee should bow, of things in heaven, and things in earth, and things under the earth; And that every

tongue should confess that Jesus Christ is Lord, to the glory of God the Father" (Philippians 2:9-11).

In fulfillment of this long-promised event concerning the birth of Jesus over two thousand years ago, many Christians throughout the world will once again celebrate God's most wonderful gift to mankind on December 25th called Christmas Day. Jesus had been born into the world to save humanity, God's masterpiece, from the inherited ravages of sin and death inherited byway of Adam. The true meaning of Jesus earthly ministry will be made plain to all men in God's own time and characteristics.

The annual Christmas holiday is a very special and festive occasion in many ways, and there is a general feeling of joy in the atmosphere and a deep sense of anticipation throughout the weeks leading up to the grand celebration. More than any other time of the year, men attention is directed toward thoughts of peace, love and goodwill toward all men. It serves as a time to be reminded of the miraculous birth of our Savior, his earthly ministry, sacrificial death on the cruel cross, and his ultimate resurrection as the firstborn which slept from the dead. He was the only perfect life that had ever lived, and without doubt. His name will forever be the sweetest name I know.

If He had not come, there would be no story of his gruesome crucifixion. We would not sing "Joy to the World the Lord has Come" or "Rock of Ages" or "Beneath the Cross of Jesus" or "The Old Rugged Cross" nor could we ever sang "Jesus Paid it All." If Jesus had not come, there would be no Church, no Pastors, no Deacons, no Sunday school, and no Youth programs.

In our modern world there is less interest and attention given to the true meaning of our Lord and Savior that knew no sin but yet conquered sin that we might live. The holiday season has thus become a hectic and busy time of the year in preparation for worldly pursuits and happiness.

We would do more running around to please folk than to praise the Father. Furthermore, holiday shoppers are caught up in the last minute quest to find the perfect gift for someone special, as well as for others whose names may appear on a list of family and friends.

This special day known, as Christmas was set aside many centuries ago by Christian people who wanted to celebrate the birth of the Savior of the world. A great deal of attention was focused on the event and it became a sacred and festive religious holiday. Students of the Bible, however, point out the fact that December 25th is not the exact day on which our Lord Jesus was actually born. The Scriptures does not specifically teach that we should celebrate Jesus' birth. Instead, we are instructed to remember our Savior's death, which accomplished the redemption price for sin thereby satisfying divine justice.

The name Jesus is defined as "Jehovah-saved" and no other name in the history of the world can ever claim such depth of meaning. It clearly points to the Master as the only one who could serve as the agency of Our Heavenly Father in the ultimate implementation of mankind's salvation. The scriptures clearly teach, *"Neither is there salvation in any other: for there is none other name under heaven given among men, whereby we must be saved"* (Acts 4:12).

This name Jesus is so sweet; a Christian in Indiana decided to identify the incarnated Jesus as a candy cane:

The Legend of the Candy Cane:

A candy maker in Indiana wanted to make a candy that would help us remember who Christmas is really about. So he made a Christmas candy cane. He incorporated several symbols for the birth, ministry, and death of Jesus Christ.

1) He began with a stick of pure white, hard candy. The white to symbolize the virgin birth and sinless nature of Jesus.

a. Mary was pure because she knew not a man before the birth of Jesus.

b. The perfect and pure life of Christ was living proof that we can also be pure. He lived in the flesh but did not give himself to the impure desires of the flesh. He never sinned!

2) Hard candy to symbolize that he's our solid rock, the foundation of the Church, and firmness of the promises of God.

a. He's our Rock in a weary land. Whenever we hit rock bottom in our lives, we too can recognize after reaching rock bottom, that he'll be the rock waiting at bottom.

b. We can stand upon his word as a solid foundation knowing that he's not slack concerning his promises.

3) The candy maker made the candy cane in the form of a "**J**" to represent the name of Jesus. It also represented the staff of the "Good Shepherd."

a. There's no other name underneath Heaven than Jesus whereby men might be saved.

b. He uses his staff to rescue us from the ditches of Life.

The candy maker then included red stripes. He used three small stripes and a large red stripe to represent the suffering Christ endured at the end of his life.

The red stripes represent the Blood He shed for us!

"But he was wounded for our transgressions, he was bruised for our iniquities: the chastisement of our peace was upon him; and with his stripes we are healed" (Isaiah 53:5).

The candy became known as the candy cane—a decoration seen at Christmas time. The meaning has faded, but still gives joy to children young and old whom Jesus loves and treasures.

In conclusion, I want to remind you that in a few months from now most of the gifts you buy this Christmas will be forgotten. The thrill of the newness of them will be lost. And probably some of them will be thrown away because they got broke.

So rather than focusing on the gifts let me encourage you to celebrate the perfect gift of Jesus Christ. Jesus Christ really is the only perfect gift; because once you meet him you will never forget him. And you will never lose the thrill of knowing him. But greatest of all, Jesus will last forever.

So each time you pay for a gift this Christmas, think about the price God paid in order that he could give you the gift of salvation. As you wrap those gifts think about God's gift of Jesus, the incarnate God, coming to this earth wrapped in flesh. And as you receive your Christmas gifts; be reminded that all you have to do to be saved is to receive the greatest gift of all, God's son, the Lord Jesus Christ.

Chapter 6

⤜✠⤝

It's not all about us; it's about Him

(John 4:23-24 KJV)
But the hour cometh, and now is, when the true worshippers shall worship the Father in spirit and in truth: for the Father seeketh such to worship him. God is a Spirit: and they that worship him must worship him in spirit and in truth.

I would like to raise an important question! When will the Church, the body of baptized believers, the regenerated soul, the kingdom of God, the bible toting, Holy Ghost filled, finite humanistic being of God, realize that when we come together to worship! That's it not all about us; but it's about Him?

One of the most solemn and soul-destroying fallacies of the day is that unregenerate souls are capable of worshipping God. Probably one chief reason why this error has gained so much ground is because of the wide-spread ignorance which it obtains concerning the real nature of true worship.

In order to worship God, he must be known: and He cannot be known apart from Christ. Much may be predicated and believed about a theoretical or a theological "God," but He cannot be known apart from our Savior.

Jesus once said, "*I am the way, the truth, and the life; no man cometh unto the Father but by me*" (John 14:6). Therefore it is a sinful make-believe, a fatal delusion, a wicked embarrassment, to cause unregenerate people to imagine that they can worship God. While the sinner remains away from Christ, he is the "enemy" of God, a child of wrath. How then can he worship God? While he remains in his unregenerate state he is "dead in trespasses and sins"; how then can he worship God.

To the Samaritan woman our blessed Lord declared, "*The hour cometh, and now is, when the true worshippers shall worship the Father in spirit and in truth; for the Father seeketh such to worship Him*" (John 4:23). And how did the Father "seek" worshippers? At the beginning of the chapter the Son of God is seen taking a journey (vv. 3, 4). His object was to seek out one of His lost sheep, to reveal Himself to a soul that knew Him not, to wean her from the lusts of the flesh, and fill her heart with His satisfying grace; and this, in order that she might meet the longings of Divine love and give in return that praise and adoration which only a saved sinner can give.

I. The Authenticity of True Worship:

People imagine that if they attend a religious service, are reverent in their demeanor, join in the singing of the old fashion hymns, listen with their undivided attention to the preacher, and support the church byway of stewardship according to (Malachi 3:10), that they have really worshipped God. Poor deluded souls, a delusion which is helped forward by the priest-craft and preacher-graft of the day. Over against this delusion are the words of Christ in (John 4:24), which are startling in their plainness and pungency: "God is Spirit; and they that worship Him must worship Him in spirit and in truth."

All too often, praise to God is something that many people leave at church, an event that happens only when they come together with other Christians. However, praise should be a part of a believer's lifestyle, inter-mingled as a part of their daily prayer-life. At work, in the car, at home in bed, or anywhere; praise to the Lord brings the refreshing of the Lord's presence, along with His power and anointing. "*I will bless the LORD at all times: his praise shall continually be in my mouth*" (Psalms 34:1).

II. The Adoration of True Worship:

Have you ever noticed a feeling inside, like a hole that you can't quite fill up? You buy a nice car, house, etc., you get a good job, wife, and kids. And still the feeling persists; like there just has to be more. So, you pay attention to that hole trying to figure out how to fill it? But nothing seems to be the right size or shape to fill that empty hole.

The reason why is because it's a God shaped hole that only a relationship with Him can fill. Once you get to know Him the hole is filled to over flowing, and the love for Him that over flows from your heart gets expressed as worship. We don't worship because we have to, we worship because we want to, and we don't die for Him! Because He died for us!

"Worship" is the new nature in the creature stirred into activity, turning to its Creator and heavenly source. Jesus demonstrated in scripture the importance of worship and how to get a breakthrough. The one true and living God is the proper object of Worship.

Christ allowed men to worship Him:

- The Wise Men Worshipped Him: Matthew 2:11
- The Leper Worshipped Him: Matthew 8:2
- The Ruler Worshipped Him: Matthew 9:18
- His Disciples Worshipped Him: Matthew 14:33
- The Woman of Canaan worshipped him: Matthew 15:25
- The Mother of Zebedee's children worship Him: Matthew 28:10

- The Mary Magdalene who had gone to the tomb worshiped Him: Matthew 28:10
- The eleven disciples worshiped Him: Matthew 28:17
- The blind man whom Jesus healed worshiped Him: John 9:38

Although men worshiped Him, Jesus taught that men are to worship the Father in Heaven (John 4:23-24).

III. The Advantages of True Worship:

Worship sends the enemy running. The devil desires worship and he gets it even today. There is a church of Satan and it was started by Anton Szandor Levay. Its official creed book is the Satanic Bible. There incorporated within are black pages with white writing. It has the satanic nine commandments. It was organized as a cult; and is an active worshiping group that is ever growing.

The Church of Satan does not solicit membership. Those who wish to affiliate can become a Registered Member for a one-time registration fee of two hundred dollars in United States currency. Affiliates receive a red card declaring them as a member of the Church of Satan to other members.

As God's Children we recognize that, praise and worship manifests God's presence, we also realize that praise and worship repels the presence of the enemy, Satan. An atmosphere which is filled with sincere worship and praise to God by humble and contrite hearts is disgusting to the Devil. He fears the power in the name of Jesus, and flees from the Lord's habitation in praise. "*Whoso offereth praise glorifieth me: and to him that ordereth his conversation aright will I show the salvation of God*" (Psalms 50:23).

When the children of Judah found themselves outnumbered by the hostile armies of Ammon, Moab, and mount Seir, King Jehoshophat and all the people sought the Lord for His help. The Lord assured the people that this would be His battle. He told them to go out against them, and

He would do the fighting for them. So what did the children of Judah do? Being the people of "praise" (Judah actually means Praise), and knowing that God manifests His power through praise, they sent their army against their enemies, led by the praisers!

So they went ahead of the army declaring, "Praise the Lord, for His mercy endureth forever!" And the scripture says, "*And when they began to sing and to praise, the LORD set ambushments against the children of Ammon, Moab, and mount Seir, which were come against Judah; and they were smitten*" (2 Chronicles 20:22).

When God's people begin to praise His name, it sends the enemy running! I challenge you to become a person of praise and worship, and you will experience the release of the power of God! God instituted worship, not man. Even Jesus said, "*I tell you that, if these should hold their peace, the stones would immediately cry out*" (Luke 19:40).

Even the earth praises God. God seeks those who worship Him. He will not make you worship. But! One day, though, every knee shall bow and every tongue shall confess that Jesus Christ is Lord.

Chapter 7

ᴄᴍ

He Saw the Best in Me

(John 15:13 KJV)
*"Greater love hath no man than this, that a man lay
down his life for his friends."*

In the text one thing is on Jesus' mind, and that's soon he will be suffering and dying. It was just before the Passover Feast. The Passover is when Israel remembered how all those in Egypt with the blood of the lamb were saved from the Lord's avenging angel.

The lamb will soon be sacrificed. Of course, the Lamb is not a little bundle of wool. Rather, it's Christ! Remember the words of John the Baptist (John 1:29) *"The next day John seeth Jesus coming unto him, and saith, Behold the Lamb of God, which taketh away the sin of the world."* He didn't have to die for our sake, but He did it! Why? He saw the best in us. Let's perform an autopsy on His life and legacy to see just how much he loved us.

I. He Exemplified His Love:

Great thinkers of the past said, "It takes as much courage to live for your friends as it does to die for them." We're talking about love; but it would require courage to die for friends even though that courage was motivated by love. By dying for a friend, we prove our love with the ultimate sacrifice; we've sealed that testimony with our blood. However, when living for a friend it requires us to be committed to that friend. If one is surprisely confused over the definition of true friendship; we can look to the Saviors life for his expressible examples.

Jesus' love attributes are self evident from the first page of the New Testament to the last. He was committed to his disciples and to those he was trying to save. In fact, He served them rigorously throughout the course of his ministry.

One great example is the washing of the disciple's feet. In Eastern custom and culture, foot-washing was an act of utter humiliation. In Israel foot-washing was considered such a degrading act; that no Hebrew slave could ever be required to perform it. But! A Gentile slave might be advised to perform the dirty work So, Jesus often performed acts that of a slave. Why? He saw the best in us.

He always cared for his friends, and personally mourned for their well beings. In fact, when Christ heard that John the Baptist was jailed, "He saw the best in John" and strengthens him by endorsing, *"John I am the one, and there's no need to look for another."* After he heard that John the Baptist was beheaded, He mourned for him. Then in the middle of His mourning and desire to be alone he preached to a multitude that followed him. Love and service!

If we could be that type of friend to our friends then we could have a serious impact on them for good. That's what Christianity is all about! Whether we die or live for our friends it is a testimony of our love for them. If they can feel that love then we have succeeded.

II. He Exhibited His Loyalty:

We live in a world where selfishness seems to be the rule of the day; and personal gain the objective of most relationships and endeavors. One of the most honorable character traits a person can develop is the ability to be loyal, whether to family, friends, an employer, or clubs and organizations to which we may belong.

There are too many fair weather friends these days that pretend to be loyal! There are too many people, who will only stick with you when things are perfect. The next minute when things change, they take off. They bad mouth you. In fact, they'll join others to run you out of town.

I can't think of a better place that this plays out than in the sports world! Listen, one moment you are the hero. A couple of weeks later after a couple of bad games everybody is booing you. We need friends like Jesus who are loyal to us for the long haul. We need people who will be by our sides who are committed to stick with us.

Jesus clearly recognized that His call and commission of loyalty came from His Father. They seemed to ring in His ears at all times; and kept His attention focused upon the will of God. Often words dropped from His lips, showing how divinely centered His mind was. And what pleasure and comfort He received from the contemplation of His heavenly call.

- *Jesus saith unto her, Woman, what have I to do with thee? mine hour is not yet come* (John 2:4).
- *Jesus answered and said unto them, "Destroy this temple, and in three days I will raise it up"* (John 2:19).
- *And as Moses lifted up the serpent in the wilderness, even so must the Son of man be lifted up* (John 3:14).
- *"I must work the works of him that sent me, while it is day: the night cometh, when no man can work"* (John 9:5).
- *Therefore doth my Father love me, because I lay down my life, that I might take it again. No man taketh it from me, but I lay it down of myself. I have power to lay it down, and I have power to take it again. This commandment have I received of my Father"* (John 10:17-18).

He was loyal even unto His death:

- Loyalty is unwavering in good times and bad (Proverbs 17:17).

35

- Loyalty is what you do, not what you say (Matthew 26:33-35 and 26:69-75).
- Loyalty is in your heart. It is willing and not reluctant (Psalm 78:8).
- Loyalty can be demanding (Exodus 17:8-13).
- Loyalty involves sacrifice (2 Chronicles 11:13-16).

III. He Exchanged His Life:

He left the comfort of Heaven, used a manger as a crib; and grew to suffer the agony of a thorny crown and scourging whip. Wait one minute! He was nailed to a wooden cross and displayed like a bloody billboard on Golgotha's hill.

In light of the whipping, thorns in his head, nails through his wrists and feet, it did not kill him. Neither did the slow suffocation on the cross. Jesus could have stepped off the cross at any moment. His crucifixion was equivalent of someone bending over and putting their head under water and choosing to deliberately drown; when they possessed the power to raise their head at any moment. Jesus chose to die.

He was very clear about this. Jesus said He was choosing to lay down His life. Jesus said, *"Greater love hath no man than this, that a man lay down his life for his friends"* (John 15:13).

Why? Because He looked at our hearts, our actions, and saw us as sick, needy, weak, sinful, blind and lost. This was Jesus' stated view of us which we don't like. But you also need to see His actions about it. It's not distant judgment or condemnation. It's not uninvolved, nor unsympathetic.

Whether you agree with him or not, He saw us desperately in need. He saw our lives as not working properly. Not living in fullness or living out the goodness He created us for. He saw us at risk of dying eternally separated from him. He saw us never to experience eternal life. He saw us cut off from him by our sin nature and chose to meet our need.

This is the greatest expression of human love:

The love that Jesus had for us goes a step beyond the unawares. Jesus did not lay His life down for His friends only, but He laid His life down for his enemies. To know Christ will increase our love for Christ. When we begin to understand the glory of His person and the wonder of his work, we will love Him more, and the more you love Him, the more you will obey Him. The more you obey Him, the more you will abide in Him, and the more you abide, the more fruit you will bear.

Ultimately to know Christ is to spend time with Christ. If we are going to be fruitful then we must spend time with Christ and obey His commandment to love one another. Ask God to help you demonstrate love and needs of people around you each day. Be obedient to help others in whatever way you are capable of helping. Ask God to show you who the people are that He want you to invest love and loyalty in. And remember, "Jesus saw the best in us."

Chapter 8

⚓

Get Your Mind Right

(James 4:7-8 KJV)
Submit yourselves therefore to God. Resist the devil, and
he will flee from you. Draw nigh to God, and he will
draw nigh to you. Cleanse your hands, ye sinners; and
purify your hearts, ye double minded.

We have had the great privileges of celebrating the Lord's Supper in the past. We have celebrated God's forgiving love in the past. Now I'm bescheeching every believer to live as saved and forgiven people—James this great vessel of God, as you know, speaks as a servant of the Lord Jesus Christ to diligent believers of the faith. In other words, his audience is those considered to be servants of God and of the Lord Jesus Christ. They have been saved and forgiven by the blood of Jesus.

In our Bible reading before us, James talks to those who are double-minded (James 4:8). This is not the only time he has used this phrase. In chapter one, James says some Christians are double-minded when it comes to prayer (James 1:8). They believe God answers prayer and yet they doubt God answers prayer. They ask God for wisdom, yet they also depend upon human wisdom. One moment they trust and believe in God; the next moment they rely on self.

These people are like the wave of the sea, blown and tossed by the wind. James is thinking of waves on the Sea of Galilee. One moment the wave is driven North, South, East, West, or cross roads in-between; and then the next moment it is driven in the exact opposite direction. Those who are double-minded are like the waves of the sea.

The Bible is filled with stories of double-minded people. I think of Jacob who pretended to be Esau and stole his brother's birthright. I think of Abraham who used his wife's maidservant to father a child. I think of David who grabbed his neighbor's wife and had her husband killed. I think of Peter who denied knowing the Lord when faced with danger. I think of Israel at the time of Elijah and Ahab.

If there ever were a people who were double-minded, it was Israel limping between two opinions; Israel tried to follow Baal and God; they tried to serve Baal and God; they bowed in worship before Baal and God. These are God's people we are talking about. Yet, they are double-minded.

Is it any different today? Regrettably no, in much of the world today it is difficult to observe any difference between those who call themselves Christians and those who are not Christians. Different surveys show that many church members are double-minded, professing faith in Christ while embracing the lifestyle of this fallen world.

Did you know, for instance, that the divorce rate among Christians is exactly the same as among those who are not Christians? Did you know that Christian teens and adult singles have pre-marital sex almost as much as non-Christian teens and adult singles? Did you know that Christians have the same problem with controlling the tongue as the unbeliever? Did you know that Christians exalt rich people and cater to them in much the same way as the world does?

Did you know that many Christians have the same problems with anger management as those in the world? Did you know that many Christians have alcohol and drug problems, just like many in the world?

Did you know that Christians, like many in the world, are not able to exercise self-control? James has expressed concern about most of this double-mindedness in the course of his letter. We claim to confess Christ. Yet, we act like the unsaved out in the world. That is what James means by "double-minded."

Now, let's be honest. To a certain extent each one of us has areas of life in which we are double-minded. I have that problem and you have that same problem for time to time. We claim to be Christians but we don't act like Christians in every area of life. We are that way because we don't really want to put every area of our life under the control of the Holy Ghost. We are that way because we all have some reluctance to be full doers of God's Word.

To be honest it's not hard being a Christian, we make it hard to be pleasing to God, and to live a life of true holiness! And I don't know about anyone else, but we must have the mind-set to live right. If perhaps we live right, I know that we will die right, and live with the Lord around His heavenly throne for eternity.

I suppose that every Christian longs to travel on the high road to holiness, blessing and victory, but there are many detours, road blocks and potholes along the way. However, in the mercy of God, He has provided certain signposts, along the high road, to get us on the right road, and to keep us on the right road. One such signpost is found in our text of (James 4: 8) "*Draw nigh to God, and He will draw nigh to you.*"

Billy Graham tells of a time, during the early years of his preaching ministry, when he was due to lead a crusade meeting in a town in South Carolina, and he needed to mail a letter. He asked a little boy in the main street how he could get to the post office. After the boy had given him directions, Billy said, "If you come to the Central Baptist Church tonight, I'll tell you how to get to heaven." The boy replied, "No thanks, you don't even know how to get to the post office!" My Point is this "A whole lot of folk try to tell others individuals how to get to heaven, and haven't figured out the true directions for themselves; *"they have zeal of God but not according to knowledge."*

James uses some graphic language and imagery, in our text, to make us aware of the fact that as we travel God's highway of holiness, there are no left turns along the way, only right turns. In other words, we are to get right, stay right and be right if God is to be our travelling companion, and when we get tired on this journey, God has a way of reviving us. If you desire to be revived in the Lord, sometimes a good one on one revival with the Lord will put you back on the tracks of righteousness.

I once heard a story about a man who once asked an evangelist, how to have a revival. The evangelist asked, "Do you have a place where you can pray?" The man answered that he did. "Tell you what you do," the evangelist said. "You go to that place, and take a piece of chalk along. Kneel down there, and with the chalk, draw a complete circle all around you. Then pray for God to send a revival to everything inside of the circle. Stay there until He answers and you will have true revival." The evangelist knew that true revival begins in the heart of each person.

If you want to change the world, start with yourself. If you want to improve the church, start with yourself. If you want Christians to fully live for Jesus, start with yourself. Because repentance always starts with self!

Those who are servants of God and of the Lord Jesus Christ, those who have taken the Lord's Supper and been reminded of God's love, need to follow James' divine constructive criticism. They need to turn from sin and to God. They need to resist the devil and submit to God.

But we don't have to do this on our own. In fact, we can't do this on our own. None of us have it within ourselves to stop our sin, our evil, our double-mindedness. None of us have the power, the self-control, and the spiritual fortitude, to totally resist the devil and turn to God. And, if we do rely on our own strength, we can only expect to fall, again and again.

However, if we humble ourselves before the Lord and rely on His power and His strength and His Spirit, He will give us His grace. That is God's promise through James (James 4:6) but he gives us more grace. That is why Scripture says: "*God opposes the proud but gives grace to the humble*" (James 4:10). Humble yourselves before the Lord, and he will lift you up.

The best example here, of course, is Jesus. He humbled Himself. He did not grasp His equality with God. He made Himself nothing. He took the nature of a servant. He was made in human likeness. He became obedient to death, even death on a cross (Philippians 2:6-8). He relied on God. So He was able to resist the devil and his temptations in the wilderness. He was able to resist the devil and the devil fled from him.

As Christians we need to realize that a godly life is characterized by its conflicts with sin and the devil. It isn't the man or woman of the world who has conflict with sin and the devil. But the Christian! The Christian should be in a state of perpetual conflict.

As fallen creatures in a fallen world, we all are double-minded. The question is, do we like this or do we fight this? Do we submit ourselves to God and resist the devil or do we submit ourselves to the devil and resist God? Do we follow James' request for repentance? "Get Your Mind Right!"

Chapter 9

⌒⁂⌒

No Weapons Shall Prosper

(Isaiah 54:17 KJV)
No weapon that is formed against thee shall prosper;
and every tongue that shall rise against thee in judgment
thou shalt condemn. This is the heritage of the servants
of the LORD, and their righteousness is of me, saith the
LORD.

In the book of Isaiah chapters 54-66; it contains massive words of comfort and assurance for the Babylonian captives who experienced God's judgment foretold in the first half of the book. The focus is mostly on the future glory of God's people, yet also with a reminder that their present captivity was due to their own wickedness and selfishness.

The Lord promises to show mercy and a covenant of peace to the faithful remnant. An invitation is given to all who thirst, and people are encouraged to seek the Lord while He may be found if they desire joy and peace.

Their idolatry had profited them nothing and cost them everything. Yet those who were humble and contrite would experience God's mercy if they would cast away hypocritical formalism and return to their true religion. Rebuking them for their sins; Isaiah then joins with them in confessing their sins.

In response, the Lord promises salvation through a Redeemer who will come to Zion and to those who turn from their transgression. Again, this is looking forward not just to their restoration from Babylonian captivity; but also to the coming of Jesus Christ who would bring full redemption through His blood.

It seems as if the world like Israel is living off the umbilical card of Satan. They have failed to realize that he has sat them in the chair of self denial and has fed them from the bowl of darkness and spoon of iniquity. And after the great feeding he wipes their mouths with the baby bips of confusion.

He has guided their hands to help them practice the steps of unrighteousness. And these individual when they have failed to follow the oracles of God, will grow up and cause the church a great injustice. These are those in which the church must withstand and realize that, "*Ye are of God, little children, and have overcome them: because greater is he that is in you, than he that is in the world*" (1 John 4:4). We must continue to stand upon our beliefs and exercise our faith that defeat is not an option.

We live in a day and age where the Christian faith is being attacked on almost every street corner of every city and every continent in the world. In the text Israel is being held captive but they have Christian faith. Seriously, they have smelled the stanch of their own waywardness. And have decided to follow the assurance of God's promise to be delivered.

But! It's not easy as spoken to free stand as one nation again. Their enemies have prepared weapons of mass destruction to keep them bound. This will disallow a successful escape; but little did the Babylonians know, "God was on the Israelites side."

Have you ever wanted to be free from the captives of life? When was your turning point? This is a serious question! Whatever has deemed you powerless; there's always a divine timing for your turn-around. There is a time appointed for your release. It is now! The case for your total emancipation from captivity is not subject to probability. It is certain!

It is a matter of time and the time is now. No weapons against you as God's child shall prosper! No enemy of God's church can prevail and as Christians we should never compromise our: Our Message, Our Methods, nor Our Master.

I. The Attack on Our Message:

The priority program of the church until Jesus returns is the communication of the Christian gospel to every creature in every country. The Master said, "Go therefore and make disciples of all the nations, baptizing them in the name of the Father and of the Son and of the Holy Spirit, teaching them to observe all things that I have commanded you; and lo, I am with you always, even to the end of the age" (Matthew 28:19-20).

Therefore, the Christian life has a very high and elevated purpose here on earth. Our message should bring glory to Jesus Christ and a testimony to everyone around. And this is only possible when the believer places himself under the obedience of God's word. If every believer would make his objective to accomplish this, most of the problems within our communities, cities, states and our nation would begin to deteriorate.

The troubles around us will never cease, because Satan will remain the ruler of this world until Jesus Christ returns to set up His Kingdom, but the problems would become more manageable. We must inform Satan that if and when he attacks our messages; he can't steal our joy and he can't borrow it either! Satan hates evangelism and discipleship, and will throw every obstacle he can in the way of missionaries and people with a zeal for evangelism.

On another note, some of the most powerful weapons in Satan's arsenal are psychological. Among these weapons are fear, doubt, anger, hostility, worry, and of course, guilt. We should be well-aware of the various ways in which Satan works. He attacks believers when he thinks it will be to his advantage.

This includes the time after a great spiritual experience, or right before someone is going to begin a new spiritual venture. He also attacks when believers are vulnerable either physically or mentally. Satan also likes to attack believers when they are alone. Christians, therefore, must always be on guard.

Satan's goal in your life:

- He wants to control you without you knowing it;
- He wants make the crooked look straight;
- He wants to snare you or trap you and bind you making you ineffective for Kingdom work;
- He wants to make you behave like him;
- He wants to lead you into greater levels of darkness;
- He wants to kill and destroy everything in your life including you.

But, even these weapons shall not prosper against you!

II. The Attack on Our Methods:

Why is it every time I turn around it looks as if Satan has singled me out? I don't mess with anybody. I try to treat everybody right; and I try to live right! If it wasn't bad luck, I wouldn't have any luck. Why Me?

Everyone at some point in life asked the question; God how can you say, "No weapons shall prosper against us?" Paul suffered on several occasions, and in the end was beheaded for his faith. John ended up on the isle of Patmos for the testimony of Jesus Christ. Early saints in the New Testament were covered with tar and oil and then set on fire and used for lighting in the arenas; still others were torn asunder by ravenous beasts in those same arenas. John Huss was burned at the stake because he took a stand on truth. Calvin had to flee from France to save his life. One could go on and on both from Scriptures and from history. Doesn't it sounds like a contradiction when God says, "No weapon formed against you shall prosper?"

Satan uses quite a collection of weapons against the godly methods of life. His attacks are highly specialized. He always uses "the effective weapon of choice." His objective is always the same in each situation and he does as much damage as possible. He does not use the same weapon against every godly person.

Godly individuals exist in a variety of different circumstances. Satan rarely attacks anyone with a weapon he knows that will be ineffective. His purpose in the attack is to create distressful temptation and struggle. But remember, "It's only a test!" And we must use prayer as our weapon to fight back against him.

Satan is persistent and will not give up until God sees that the result of the test is successful. (Job 42:10) *And the LORD turned the captivity of Job, when he prayed for his friends: also the LORD gave Job twice as much as he had before.* You may have to endure a test of some length of time before the desired result may be achieved. Sometimes the result God seeks in your life might just be an outward testimony to others of the keeping power of God through hostile circumstances. Sometimes it will seem that right around every corner there is another satanic hindrance to your Christian walk. This need not cause us to walk crookedly in our walk. If we are covered by the blood of Jesus, Satan's weapons will be classified as ineffective.

But! We ought to never doubt Satan's ability to choose an effective weapon! Peter was one of Jesus' "inner circle" apostles. God revealed to him that Jesus was the Christ (Matthew 16:17). Even the other eleven did not understand that truth! Peter was the confident champion of Jesus the Messiah. The last night of Jesus' earthly life, Jesus told Peter that he would deny Him that night (Matthew 26:34).

Oh no not bold Peter! Peter was certain death itself could not make him deny Jesus (Matthew 26:33-35)! Yet, before daylight, Peter said, not once but three times, that he did not know Jesus (Matthew 26:75).

How could "the impossible" happen? Did Satan use alcohol, drugs, a seductive woman, greed, or jealousy? No. In that situation, those were ineffective weapons. Ineffective weapons would strengthen Peter, and that was not Satan's goal! Satan used an effective weapon, a weapon Peter regarded. He was strong! He was sacrificial! He paid great prices to follow Jesus!

III. The Attack on Our Master:

According to Jesus' wilderness temptation (Matthew 4:1-11); it is easy to see that Satan attacked our Master in some way and that he had a very intense hatred toward Him. But it is not entirely clear why Satan is chose to attack Jesus in specific ways. It is clear that Satan tried to make Jesus sin, but Satan was never able to get any victory over Him.

Satan fights a very legal battle. It is easy to see that he was not trying to destroy Jesus physically. He wasn't allowed to hurt Jesus in anyway. So Satan had to try to conduct a legal war by getting Jesus to sin against God. It's the only way that Satan could try to get back at God.

Satan lost his battle against Jesus but that did not stop him. He is now continuing his war by attacking Christ's followers. He claims this world as his and he expects all on this world to follow him, including Christ's followers. But they are decided followers of Jesus and will not follow him at all.

All in this world belongs to Jesus. It's his; earth is his lodge, and heaven his home. This life is his, with all its sorrows and its joys; death is his, with all its terrors and solemn realities; and eternity is his, with all its immortality and its grandeur. God is his, with all his attributes. We are co-heirs and joint-heirs with him as the Son of God. Whatever we need Jesus have it!

In conclusion, in the midst of our shouting, some of us must ask the simple question, "What does this mean?" Some of us make a simple statement that if our enemies' weapons cannot hurt the true child of God. In this world the righteous are a bit like Superman. The wicked shoot guns at the righteous but the bullets simply fall down. Knives don't cut the child of God and the weapons of evil doers are rendered useless in their presence.

Yes today weapons may overtake us. Yes today weapons may hurt us. Yes today you are hurt. But this vision of the future lets us know that is not God's ultimate intention. This text lets us know that a day is coming when the "wicked shall cease from troubling and the weary shall be at rest." And when God's ultimate intention is fully realized, "we will study war no more."

Chapter 10

⌒⁓

I'm Black and I'm Proud

(Exodus 1:11-14 KJV)
Therefore they did set over them taskmasters to afflict them with their burdens. And they built for Pharaoh treasure cities, Pithom and Raamses. But the more they afflicted them, the more they multiplied and grew. And they were grieved because of the children of Israel. And the Egyptians made the children of Israel to serve with rigour: And they made their lives bitter with hard bondage, in morter, and in brick, and in all manner of service in the field: all their service, wherein they made them serve, was with rigour.

Thousands of years ago, according to the Old Testament, the Jews were slaves in Egypt. The Israelites had been in Egypt for generations, but now that they had become so numerous; the Pharaoh feared their presence. He feared that one day the Israelites would turn against the Egyptians. Gradually and stealthily, he forced them to become his slaves. He made the slaves build grand "treasure cities." The Egyptian overseers were given instructions to oversee and keep watch on top of a tower, while the slaves make bricks from clay and straw.

The Israelites had to work long and hard at making building bricks for the Egyptians. At one point, the Pharaoh ruled that if a man didn't meet his quota of bricks for the day that his baby was to be put into the buildings instead of bricks. This kind of persecution got worse. The king pharaoh was afraid of a prophecy that foretold of a deliverer for the Hebrew people. So the pharaoh ordered that all of the baby boys be thrown in the river from then on.

In this twenty first century in which we live, we have to endorse poetic Solomon the black son of David who indicated in scriptures; there's nothing new that happens under the sun. Furthermore, that which happened in the past has its formatical directional ways of appearing in the future.

I. The Struggles of the Afro-Americans:

The man and woman of color have always faced rejection because of their skin complexion. Matter of fact many in the pass faced massive persecution and were treated with less respect than that of a dog infected with rabies and oozing mange. Our ancestors identified and experienced the hostile environment of the slave master, but through these difficult, disastrous, demeaning, diabolical, distasteful, dilemmas; they were determined no matter how long it would take. To fight for freedom and equality!

Many slaves were considered house slaves. To serve as a house slaves you had no free time at all and was always on call. Some owners even expected their house slaves to sleep at the foot of their beds in case they wanted something at night. Some house slaves deliberately did badly at housework so that they would be sent back to the fields with those they were familiar with no matter how hard the task was to be completed.

The system of plantation slavery in the South was barbaric. Moreover while being transported out their native land of Africa, many of them died aboard the slaving ships, packed aboard them like cattle; during the middle passage from Africa to America. Furthermore, those who survived the transition were stripped of their rights under the planters' guns and the overseers' whips.

Many have written and argued that slavery was a sin of the South. I would argue most strongly that slavery was not a sin of the South; it was the sin of a Nation. Placing the sin of slavery onto the doorstep of the confederacy is easy, and even comforting, but unfortunately is not the complete picture. The simple picture of slavery as a Southern sin does not reflect the much broader participation, exploitation and profit in slavery as an enterprise. Despite these critical dispositions the African American man and woman knew that one day God would prevail in such a way and look upon their burnt, bruised, and battled skin and set them free.

II. The Sufferings of the African Americans:

They were forbidden to speak their native African languages or practice their native customs. They were forced to labor from dawn to dusk starting as children. The Africans were literally worked to death. When they entered full-time field work, the male field hands had a life expectancy of only nine years to work and literally die after planting, plucking and plowing in the fields.

The slaves was not considered a human being by U.S. law, but merely considered to be property formerly known as black gold. The sacred slave marriages were not recognized to be sacred, because aggressively the slave masters commonly took advantage of the black slave women.

When the slave women delivered a child; their children were sold away from their parents and husbands from their wives. They could not travel without a pass and were forbidden to learn how to read or write or to hold meetings without supervision. The slave masters could beat, torture, whip their slaves, and even kill them without punishment and the threat of going to prison.

Slave foods were also dehumanizing but God (Jehovah Jireh) provided a meal out of what the master called mess! For example:

After a pig was butchered, the best parts were kept and the remaining of the pigs was thrown out for the slaves to consume. They knew how to survive off what we call soul food.

- Chittlins were pig intestines that were cleaned and boiled;
- Hog Maws were pig stomachs that was cleaned and boiled;
- Pig feet's was something the pigs used to walk around on were clean and pickled for a good day's meal;
- Hog head cheese was the (Pig's head);
- Barbeque pork ribs (the rib cage of the Pig);
- Barbeque beef ribs (the rib cage of the Cow);
- Lobsters (The slave masters taught that lobsters were an insult to eat and gave them to the slaves to eat, but now It's a delicate food);
- Boiled upside down chicken feet was a desired favorite;
- Fried Tomatoes;
- Clay Dirt (eating this became a custom among slaves).

Slavery as a legal institution lasted for about 250 years up until the *Emancipation Proclamation* of 1865 and for another 100 years, African Americans were subjected to Jim Crow laws of which they were not seen as legally equal until 1965. Initially, reparations were to be paid by giving freed slaves 40 acres of land and a mule, but the bill was vetoed by President Andrew Johnson in 1869 after having passed in Congress.

If the truth be told many of our Presidents owned and also treated the slaves as valuable compromising property. On American paper currency many Presidents had some form of connection to Slavery:

- **George Washington** on the $1.00 bill was a slave owner;
- **Thomas Jefferson** on the $2.00 bill was a slave owner;
- **Abraham Lincoln's** on the $5.00 bill his wife Mary Todd Lincoln was from a family who were slave owners;
- **Alexander Hamilton** on the $10.00 bill was in the shipping of slave's business;
- **Andrew Jackson** on the $20.00 bill was a slave owner;

- **U.S. Grant** on the $50.00 bill, wife was a slave owner;
- **Benjamin Franklin** on the $100.00 bill was in the slave trading business.

If slavery is the "be all end all" issue that defines US history, then why not revise all US paper currency. After all it state legibly on the bill "In God We Trust."

III. The Segregation of the Afro Americans:

Over a century after the abolition of slavery, the Afro-American people in the United States still suffer under a yoke of terrible oppression. This oppression is not disappearing—it is growing. Throughout the 60's, racism changed dramatically in a various number of ways. Changes involved the passage of bills into laws as well as involving the overall attitude of the people. Racism was largely based on Caucasians hatred towards Blacks until the 1960's, when several major events increased animosity both from whites towards blacks and from blacks towards whites.

In 1965, the Voting Rights act was passed, eliminating poll tax which is the 24th Amendment to the constitution, and literacy tests, therefore helping not just blacks, but all Americans gain equal rights. One of the biggest things that stood out about the 60's, and probably the most remembered about, was the killings of two very famous people in our American history. One of those men was the great black leader Malcolm X, who was killed on February 21, 1965.

The most influential American of the 60's was Martin Luther King, Jr. Through his preaching on non-violent protest, he also soon developed many followers, both black and white. He was put in jail several times, but managed to write a book and continue his preaching. On April 4, 1968, he fell to an assassin's bullet on the balcony of the Lorrain Motel in Memphis Tennessee.

For centuries we have been forced to live as colonized people inside the United States, victimized by the most vicious, racist system in the world. We have helped to build the most industrious country in the world. We are also not aware that the exploitation of colored people around the world is aided and abetted by white Christian churches and synagogues is only a beginning of reparations due us as people who have been exploited and degraded, brutalized, killed and persecuted.

IV. The Success of the Afro-Americans:

- **Elijah McCoy** (1843-1929) invented an oil-dripping cup for trains;
- **Lewis Latimer** (1848-1928) invented an important part of the light bulb—the carbon filament;
- **George Washington Carver** (1860-1943) invented peanut butter and 400 plant products;
- **Madam C. J. Walker** (1867-1919) invented a hair-growing lotion. Walker grew up poor. But she became the first female African—American millionaire;
- **Garrett Morgan** (1877-963) invented the gas mask. Morgan also invented the first traffic signal;
- **Otis Boykin** (1920-1982) invented the electronic control devices for guided missiles, IBM computers, and the pace-maker;
- **Andrew Beard**—Automatic Car Coupling Device (1897);
- **C. B. Brooks**—Street Sweeper (1896);
- **W. Johnson**—Egg Beater (1884);
- **J. L. Love**—Pencil Sharpener (1897);
- **Alexander Miles**—Elevator (1888);
- **W. H. Sammons**—Hot Comb (1920);
- **Dr. Daniel Hale Williams**—First Open Heart Surgery (1893);
- **J. T. White**—Lemon Squeezer (1896).

Simon of Cyrene—over Two Thousand years ago was the first Black African to carry the cross of Jesus. I'm Black and I'm Proud! What about you today? Hang on in there; a change is going come.

Chapter 11

⌒✐⌒

Get Your Shine On

(Matthew 5:14-16 KJV)
*"Ye are the light of the world. A city that is set on an hill
cannot be hid. Neither do men light a candle, and put
it under a bushel, but on a candlestick; and it giveth
light unto all that are in the house. Let your light so
shine before men, that they may see your good works, and
glorify your Father which is in heaven."*

In the text Jesus is on the mountain teaching the beatitudes. These beatitudes tells us of those who are poor, those who are hungry, those who weep, those who hearts are pure, those who work to establish peace, and those who suffer for the cause of justice. These individuals are all classified as blessed in the kingdom of God.

Then the Sermon on the Mount speaks of the response of those who are blessed. What is our responsibility? It tells us: *"You are the salt of the earth; you are the light of the world."* All who are blessed are called to a responsibility. This responsibility requires Christian discipleship, and membership in the kingdom of God.

When it comes to Jesus using the light as a metaphor, we must know the significance of it. Is there a difference between lighting a match, and lighting a candle? Is there a difference between a candle and a lamp? The significance of a match, a candle, and a lamp is most important; they all

56

give off light, but they all require someone to care for them. We don't make much use of candles and lamps. We would rather use a light bulb, you turn it on and it keeps going until it blows out and needs a replacement. But even the light bulb has someone to care for it.

Again, let it be known that light cannot be produced unless there's a power company involved. But the power company cannot be operational, unless there are some employees to maintain the generators which produce the electricity. In order for our lights to be proactive; we must be hooked up to the right power source.

Light is a very common metaphor in the Bible. Along with darkness, light is often used to contrast knowledge and ignorance. Here it almost certainly stands for the world's opportunity to perceive the truth about Jesus. The world is, "in the dark" about God, but Christians "turn on the lights." Light allows people to see. Christians allow the world to understand how much God loves them and what Jesus has done to restore their relationship with him.

I. We must be Visible Lights:
Verse 14

"Ye are the light of the world. A city that is set on an hill cannot be hid."

Our text says that we are the light of the world, since that is so, what keeps us going? If we were left here without a redeemer, who dwells amongst us and within us, byway of the third person of the God head trinity, we would then remain in an incubated stage of life. We would then rob the identity of the match; we would go out quickly.

So, who keeps us going? God keeps us going! We need to be plugged into His steady stream of grace that flows to us through our Savior. If you notice that your light is weak, perhaps it is time to ask, am I plugged into Christ? We are called upon daily to drown the darkness of our old nature. And to surface daily to the newness of life which is ours in Christ. Once that darkness is drowned, "we can get our shine on."

When we read of light and darkness, light is sight, and darkness is blindness. Furthermore, light is having wisdom, and darkness is unawareness. Another way of looking at this, if we are a light bulb, prayer is the alternating current. Prayer begins with God talking to us, God invites us, and we respond. But prayer is more than our response, it is also listening to God speak to us. If we don't listen, it's like we are only half plugged in, for it is not our words, but the grace that comes from God that gives the current. We listen to God by reading and studying His Word, the Bible. Our response to God's grace does not give light, but it does tell the light keeper, that we have received what was given and are ready to receive again.

And as good as it is to have light, for it keeps us from stumbling, shows us where we are, and guides us to where we are going. The point of the text is that when God made us light, he didn't do it just for our benefit. God made us the light of the world, and in this way we are doing exactly what Jesus did, for he also was the light of the world. He came to bring light to those sitting in darkness. He came to show the love and grace of God. He brings salvation and life. We are lights, but we cannot give life. But we can guide people to the one who does give life. We can lead people to Jesus, so that he can give them life.

II. We must be Vigilant Lights:
Verse 15

"Neither do men light a candle, and put it under a bushel, but on a candlestick; and it giveth light unto all that are in the house."

God does not hide us under a basket, but he puts us on a lamp stand, so that our light can give light to all who's watching us, and at the same time guide them to our Savior. Be ever mindful that the world is watching us. It's not that we lift up ourselves, and say, look at how great I am, look at how much better I am than you. God puts us on a pedestal, and he does it so that people can see in us, what God would do also for them. If we are on a pedestal it is important that we are a good light.

In the face of persecution, Jesus says to us, *"Don't put your light up under a bushel, but on a candlestick; and it giveth light unto all that are in the house."* a Christian might be tempted to hide their identity. But Jesus says if people don't know about our relationship with him, then it defeats the purpose of our "layover" here on earth. That's the way it is with our witness in the world. If we are going to be effective in the role that Jesus gave us as his followers, then we need to be visible and uplift an invisible God.

III. We must Vibrate Lights:
Verse 16

"Let your light so shine before men, that they may see your good works, and glorify your Father which is in heaven."

It is imperative that we execute quickly, and efficiently; positive action to get out and rub shoulders with the people of the world. Many of us work in environments everyday with unbelievers. What a great opportunity to get to know people and allow them to see the light of Jesus in us through our goodness. When Jesus left us here, that's exactly what he intended.

You see God has faith in us, and he trusts that we will be good examples, and faithful lights. And it is the grace of God that keeps us going that keeps our light brightly shining. That's why it's important that we remain plugged into the source of grace.

We should shine so that others may see our good deeds and praise God. Shining does not mean self-propaganda, self-publicity, or self-praise, but bearing fruit in our life, bringing life and light to others. It is about our deeds in this society.

Why, because this light we have been given is not just for us, but it is to bring hope to the world, showing it the way of Salvation in Jesus our Savior. It is hope because the world has seen what we were and has also seen the grace of God at work in our lives. And so we boast of God who put light into our lives, making us a new creation. And we boast of God who maintains the lights by his grace. And we boast of God who has put us on a pedestal, and enables us to be a good example and a true light. God has done all this for us in love, and so we give him thanks and praise in Jesus name. Amen!

Chapter 12

⌒୨୧⌒

There's No Place Like Home

(Genesis 33:16-20 KJV)

So Esau returned that day on his way unto Seir. And Jacob journeyed to Succoth, and built him an house, and made booths for his cattle: therefore the name of the place is called Succoth. And Jacob came to Shalem, a city of Shechem, which is in the land of Canaan, when he came from Padanaram; and pitched his tent before the city. And he bought a parcel of a field, where he had spread his tent, at the hand of the children of Hamor, Shechem's father, for an hundred pieces of money. And he erected there an altar, and called it EleloheIsrael.

In the previous chapters Jacob resided with Laban. God indeed blessed him and Jacob became wealthy. In fact, Jacob worked for Laban and in result he made Laban rich as well. He did not want Jacob to leave and rest from his labor. He specifically wanted Jacob to stay there and work for the rest of his life! He even found ways to trick Jacob so he would stay in Haran instead of going back home.

It's hilarious how God allowed Jacob to be tricked by Laban. Remember how Jacob had tricked his brother Esau to take some pottage in exchange for his birthright and trick his blind daddy Isaac for Esau's blessing? Jacob with much success got Esau to sign on the dotted line and figuratively made himself to feel superior over him.

In fact, if you researched the Hebraic name Jacob; you will discover his name means: Trickster, Conniver, or Manipulator. God sometimes lets his children experience the same bad things that they do to other people. In the story of Jacob he experienced what it felt like to be tricked. Uncle Laban had done an excellent job at that.

In one episode of Jacob life; Laban happened to have just what Jacob wanted: He wanted to take a woman's hand in marriage named Rachel (Genesis 29:15-20). Instead of giving him Rachel for free, Laban took advantage of the opportunity. He made a deal with Jacob. Does this remind you of the deal that Jacob once made with hungry Esau?

It is as if Laban was saying something like this: "Jacob, you have what I want and I have what you want. I'll give you Rachel and you give me seven years of hard work." Laban was able to get Jacob to "sign on the dotted line" and the deal was made! This again reminds us of the time Jacob forced Esau to sign on the dotted line!

Seven years seemed like nothing to Jacob (Genesis 29:20). He would gladly have "climbed the highest mountain, crossed the hottest desert and sailed the deepest ocean" for her! Oh my God, Sister Rachel was a brick house and Jacob knew she was worth working for to obtain. He would patiently and gladly put in seven years for the girl he loved!

At the end of these seven years Jacob is eighty four years old. The time has come for the wedding (Genesis 29:21-22). Instead of Laban giving him Rachel, Laban gave him popped eyed Leah. Remember during the wedding the bride is veiled! Jacob thought that it was Rachel but he was completely mistaken, and in the morning he discovered it was Leah (Genesis 29:25). Jacob was tricked by his own uncle!

There are many who scheme and connive and plot and deceive as they travel down life's road. They do this in order to try to benefit and better themselves. Instead of trusting the Lord for His best they try to work things out their way. Often they want what is good such as happiness, security, freedom, a bright future, and a good marriage. But they try to obtain what is good in the wrong way—Are you a schemer? Are you a trickster? It does not pay to scheme and Jacob had to learn this the hard way.

I. Jacob's Guilt concerning Esau:

Like Dorothy on the Wizard of Oz, Jacob has reached the crossroads of life. He has decided it was time to leave Laban's home in Haran and go back to his own home in Canaan to be with his parents. In a dream, God said, "*Go back to your own land; I will be with you*" (Genesis 31:13-16). It's been twenty years since you've messed over your own brother Esau and was sent to Haran by your mother Rebekah to keep confusion down.

So, Jacob many years later puts his children on camels, and he gathered his family and all his animals and all the other things he had gotten while he was at Laban' house in Haran, and Jacob left, heading for his father Isaac's home in the land of Canaan.

Jacob was anxious about one thing; the meeting with his brother Esau! Why was he so anxious? He remembered the things that had happened between them in the past; and wanted to make things right. Jacob was still afraid that Esau would still be angry, and he was more afraid when he heard that Esau was coming up on the eastern side of Jordan from the land of Edom, where he lived, with four hundred men. I suppose Jacob finally realized that his conspiracy in the pass caused him great guilt in the present and thought that Esau was on his way to get even. In fact, guiltiness ran in the family:

1. **Isaac his daddy was guilty.** Even though God had said that the blessing would go to Jacob, Isaac was determined to give it to his favorite son Esau (Genesis 25:28; 27:1, 4). Isaac was guilty of fighting against God's will.

2. **Rebekah his mother was guilty.** Even though Rebekah knew God's promise that Jacob (her favorite son) would be blessed, she still tried to bring this about by a deceptive scheme (Genesis

25:28; 27:6-10). She tried to get the right thing in the wrong way and she was guilty of not believing in God's promise.

3. **Jacob himself was guilty**. He went along with his mother's scheme and became a deceiver and a liar and now his guilt has caught up with him (Genesis 27:12, 19).

4. **Esau his brother was guilty**. Esau wanted the blessing that really did not belong to him and when he lost the blessing he was angry to the point of wanting to commit murder (Genesis 27:41). For a comparison (see Hebrews 12:16-17).

II. Jacob's Gratitude concerning Esau:

After Jacob found out that Esau was headed to town; he got nervous! Then Jacob did something that was very important. He prayed:

And Jacob said, O God of my father Abraham, and God of my father Isaac, the LORD which saidst unto me, Return unto thy country, and to thy kindred, and I will deal well with thee: I am not worthy of the least of all the mercies, and of all the truth, which thou hast shewed unto thy servant; for with my staff I passed over this Jordan; and now I am become two bands. Deliver me, I pray thee, from the hand of my brother, from the hand of Esau: for I fear him, lest he will come and smite me, and the mother with the children. And thou saidst, I will surely do thee good, and make thy seed as the sand of the sea, which cannot be numbered for multitude (Genesis 32:9-12).

So, after his prayer Jacob sent forward rich presents, one after another, goats and sheep and female camels, cows, bulls and asses, to meet Esau, calling Esau "my lord," and himself his servant. But Esau declined the gifts that were offered. Esau made it very clear that he was not appeased, or even impressed by Jacob's gifts. The Lord had changed Esau's heart. We don't know when this occurred. At the time Jacob fled Canaan, Esau spoke of murdering Jacob. Here we see Esau coming to meet Jacob and treating him like a brother. He made it clear; however, that Jacob hadn't even slightly impressed Esau with all the gifts and commotion.

Jacob then went himself, and his family followed in three companies (Genesis 32:13-32). When Esau saw Jacob afar off he began to run towards Jacob with swiftness. This must have given Jacob skipping heart beats.

When Jacob met his brother, he bowed seven times to him and begged him to accept the presents. It was a friendly meeting no drama involved. The two brothers embraced each other and wept. Esau went back to his home in the mountains of Edom, and Jacob crossed the Jordan to the place near Shechem where Abraham first camped. He bought a beautiful meadow and dug a well for water for his cattle. So Jacob was safe back in the land of Canaan, after his journey and his long stay in Haran. I can hear Jacob finally say, "There's No Place Like Home!"

Chapter 13

⌒*w*⌒

It's So Hard to Say Goodbye

(John 19:25-27 KJV)
*Now there stood by the cross of Jesus his mother, and his
mother's sister, Mary the wife of Cleophas, and Mary
Magdalene. When Jesus therefore saw his mother, and
the disciple standing by, whom he loved, he saith unto
his mother, Woman, behold thy son! Then saith he to the
disciple, Behold thy mother! And from that hour that
disciple took her unto his own home.*

Mother's Day is very important to acknowledge in respect to our Mother's. This great day was set aside, by President Woodrow Wilson on May 9th, 1914 when congress declared the second Sunday in May as Mother's Day. President Wilson said that this day has been set aside as a time for "public expression of our love and reverence for the mother's of our country."

This Mother's Day tribute is for us all because each of us either has or has had mothers. As with all God's best gifts, mothers too are given freely to all humanity, both rich and poor. Our mothers are special to us because out of all the people in the world, we are indebted to them for our existence and no one else loves us with that special kind of love.

God has honored mothers to be co-workers with Him in the formation of a new life. The mother's part in this work is important; she carried or carries the fetus, and supplies or supplied nutrition for the child through the umbilical cords. We are considered flesh of her flesh in this particular course work. But! This is far less than God's work in designing the child, and creating and framing together each part of the child (Psalm 139:14).

Our Mothers were marvelously designed by God both physically and mentally—to be God's co-workers in producing and bringing up children. All of us were once a part of our mothers. We all were flesh of their flesh and bones of their bones.

Therefore when a child rejects or rebels against his mother, it is extremely painful to her because she views it as her own flesh fighting against herself. When a Mother's child is dying it's as if a part of her-self is dying which makes, "It's so hard to say Goodbye."

In this chapter Jesus expressed bountiful gratitude for Mary His mother. He pauses long enough to acknowledge and encourage her amongst the crowd. He knows this hour is extremely hard for her to bear. So, He encourages his mother in his dying hour from Calvary. Calvary where there was a fountain filled with blood drawn from Emmanuel's veins, Calvary where sinners plunge beneath that flood lose all their guilty stains, Calvary where all the ransomed church of God is saved to sin no more.

Mary is older but she's at Calvary. Joseph is gone. But! She's still stands at Calvary. Her shoulders are bending beneath the burden of the many years. And there are a few silver threads taking up residence in her head. She can't move like she use to during her years of youthfulness. But she's still stands at Calvary!

At Calvary she watched as they beat him. She heard with the ear of a mother the screams, the cries of agony as she watched her son being tortured to death. She couldn't lift a finger to help him. She heard the swear words of the crowd. She watched as they walked by and slapped him and beat him with much cruelty, and cursed him. And she could do nothing about it.

Mary doesn't want his encouragement; she wants him down from that cross. Mary wants the nails withdrawn from his hands that once hugged her neck. Mary wants the rivets pulled from his feet in which she saw him take his first steps. Mary wants the crown of thorns, all seventy two of them eradicated from his brow to stop the swelling of his brain. In other words although Jesus her Son was in this condition. She thought that if she could get Him down, she could restore him. Let me insert a sidebar and say, "A Mother's work is never done."

A mother's greatest joy is her child. She loves their smile, gesture, and praises. But, Mary was persistent and concerned for her child. This was not the right time in her mind to be accepting hospitality from Jesus. She wants her child down alive from that cross.

Look at him hanging there between two worlds. He has endured:

- A Mad Monday;
- A Tearful Tuesday;
- A Wicked Wednesday;
- A Terrible Thursday;
- A Frightful Friday;
- A Silent Saturday;
- But He will rise on a Supernatural Sunday.

He turns and sees Mary his mother, and all the love she had in her heart went out to him. He then looks to John and back to Mary and says, "Woman, behold your son," He then turned to John and said, "Behold, thy mother" (John 19: 26-27).

He was saying, "John the responsibilities I have had while on earth, and the things I have done is now your responsibility." I want you to take care of my mother. I want you to do the things that I did. In an earthly way, the things that need to be taken care of, I want you to take care of them. John! My mother is a widow. She has no social security check or Medicare. Take care of her!

Jesus was the oldest son; it was his responsibility to always see that his mother was cared for. This was Jewish custom and also part of honoring one's parents in accordance with the commandment.

Jesus knew, as he hung on the cross that his death was near. He was in severe pain and knew He was about to make the ultimate sacrifice according to his heavenly Father's plan. In spite of the agony, Jesus was concerned about his mother and how she would live after he was gone. "It would be so hard to say goodbye." He made provision for his mother by charging John, whom he deeply respected and loved to take care of her as if she was his own mother. As is written in (John 19:27) Jesus' oral statement before witnesses made the obligation to John binding.

In closing, eventually every mother has to let go of her child which is the right way to raise them. Slowly they break away they leave you. First to kindergarten then to middle school before you know it they are leaving for college and then for a spouse or a career or a calling or maybe all three. The leaving, the breaking away is sometimes fast but often slow. It is the right thing but that doesn't mean it is the easiest thing. Saying farewell to being the most important person in your life is difficult. Let's admit it, "It's so hard to say Goodbye" especially to the one's you love.

Chapter 14

⟡

Forgive Your Judas'

(John 13:18 KJV)
I speak not of you all: I know whom I have chosen: but that the scripture may be fulfilled, He that eateth bread with me hath lifted up his heel against me.

A stranger may be able to hurt you, or deceive you, or beguile you; but only someone you care about deeply can betray you. A stranger does not hold your trust so they cannot betray you. In fact, you have little or nothing invested in a stranger. So you lose nothing.

In this chapter Jesus knew his betrayer. He knew what Judas was going to do. But! The impact of Judas' actions was so powerful on all of the Disciples that you cannot find any favorable words about Judas in any of the gospel accounts. He is always mentioned as the one who betrayed Jesus.

Matter of fact some of us right now feel as though we have been betrayed. But whatever side of this word you stand; I want you to observe how Jesus dealt with the subject of betrayal. I want us to look at the one who never betrays us, the one who is always faithful and true. How He deals with those who spray on a watered down characteristic of friendship. But whenever it wears off you smell the odor of betrayal.

I. The Scene before the Scandal:

It happens on a night when Jesus has thoroughly washed the grit and grim from the Disciples feet. They are enjoying the lavish Paschal meal of the Passover. They're gathered in a U-shaped, low table, sitting on the floor with their left elbows on the table. As the Disciples surround this U-shaped table, their feet are sticking out from behind the table or away from the table. And with their left elbows on the table, they're able to use their right hand to eat the meal and to drink as need be.

Jesus has positioned Himself in the base of the U, perhaps in the center position which is the place of the host. And he serves as the host at this meal. He is the one blessing and breaking the bread which is the role of the host.

There are two honored positions there at that portion of the table. There is the most honored position. And actually the most honored position is to the left. Just to the left and actually just slightly behind Jesus is the place of highest honor. And to the right of Jesus is the place of second highest honor. And Judas is sitting proudly in one of these honored seats amongst Jesus and the other Disciples.

Always remember! One thing about a betrayer, they always desire to sit in a seat of authority. Judas was a man appointed to authority but couldn't handle working as a teammate! But notice Jesus always left him along. What a shame, Judas will soon sell Jesus out for 30 pieces of silver. This was a price of a slave! And Jesus while being arrested in the Garden of Gethsemane will soon call Him a friend.

And Jesus said unto him, Friend, wherefore art thou come? Then came they, and laid hands on Jesus, and took him (Matthew 26:50).

Judas should have had more respect for Jesus as his leader. He saw Jesus give sight to one born blind. He personally witnessed the cleansing of lepers. He witnessed Jesus healing a paralyzed man in Peter's mother-in-law's home. He witnessed Jesus raise, Jairus' daughter, the widow's only son, and his friend Lazarus. He witnessed the miracle of Jesus walking on the water and then calmed the storm that was sinking their boat. He witnessed Jesus healing the demonic man in the grave yard.

He himself partook of the miraculous loaves and fishes along with thousands of others. He had even been sent forth and saw God perform miracles through his own hands—healings, and even the casting out of demons in Jesus' name. He had seen all this, and now in his heart he has decided to betray Jesus.

I dare Judas to treat Jesus with such demise and disrespect. Jesus didn't deserve this type of treatment. Not Jesus! It seem like Jesus just hospitably let Judas run over Him. I dare Judas to do my Lord this way. And Jesus calls him a friend! Surely a friend wouldn't sell you out!

II. The Suspect Exposed Secrecy:

Jesus says in verse 18, *"I speak not of you all: I know whom I have chosen: but that the scripture may be fulfilled, He that eateth bread with me hath lifted up his heel against me."*

Jesus says, "I know every one of you. I know your heart. I know what you're thinking. I know what you're planning." Now Judas has already met with the Pharisees. He's already made his deal with them for 30 pieces of silver, and no doubt he is going to point out who Jesus is.

According to Mark, the disciples desired for the betrayer to be revealed immediately:

The Lord's statement produced an emotional shock: The Disciples one by one began to ask, *"Lord, is it I?"* (Mark 14:19). "Really all of them were guilty of saying something derogative about Jesus to each other." But the traitor was revealed by methodology:

Jesus answered, He it is, to whom I shall give a sop, when I have dipped [it].
And when he had dipped the sop, he gave [it] to Judas Iscariot, [the son] of
Simon (John 13:26).

During the meal they would take a piece of bread, and they would
dip it into a bowl and grab a hold of the best thing in the bowl. And they
would sort of use the bread like a fork to grab a hold of it. And with that
morsel, they got out of the bowl, they would then hand it to someone as a
gesture of hospitality. And that is what Jesus does, and He hands this good
morsel, this gesture of hospitality, this gesture of friendship to Judas. In
other words Jesus treated Judas with kindness. That's scripture!
If thine enemy be hungry, give him bread to eat; and if he be thirsty, give him
water to drink: For thou shalt heap coals of fire upon his head, and the LORD
shall reward thee (Proverbs 25:21-22).

It's like Jesus was saying to us, "Watch the strategy of the enemy and
point them out that others will be informed to stay away from betrayers."
If you've ever been betrayed forgive your Judas. And Pray!

Every day in addition to praying for all the great people in our lives;
we must also pray for those who choose to be our enemies. We must pray
that their hard hearts will be softened, that their minds will be opened,
and that they will see the error of their ways and repent.

The statement "one of you will betray me" is meant to arrest the
attention of the disciples to drop everything, and think about what is
being said. One of you will betray me into the hands of my enemies and
have me arrested, tried, convicted, and condemned. This is Jesus final
steps that will result in the cross at Calvary.

III. The Suggestion from the Savior:

Jesus says to the betrayer:

And after the sop Satan entered into him. Then said Jesus unto him, That
thou doest, do quickly (John 13:27).

When a person is committed to betrayal, when there is no turning back; when a person is committed to a course of betrayal, sometimes the only thing you can say is; "let's hurry up and get this over with." Jesus has exhausted his appeals; all further effort would simply be a waste of time. Jesus is saying I am ready; I am ready for you to give your best shot. I am ready and I am not afraid. Jesus had come into the world to die for the sins of the world. His hour had come!

In closing, forgive your Judas and set him and yourself free. Let your Judas know that you know what he is up to and announce it to the saints, if necessary. Consider that there might be another source and motive than the devil, but do not try to judge the motive! Leave that to God! Give Him the glory and allow Him to use the stick of His choice. Heap coals of love on their heads! Try to find God's thoughts and see the big picture! Do not let bitterness rob you of the peace that comes from submission to Him and from forgiveness. Do this and you will find strength and maybe even a stronger friend than imaginable as God work in your life.

Chapter 15

⌒⁓⌒

It's Time to Cross Over

(Joshua 1:8-9 KJV)
This book of the law shall not depart out of thy mouth;
but thou shalt meditate therein day and night, that
thou mayest observe to do according to all that is written
therein: for then thou shalt make thy way prosperous,
and then thou shalt have good success. Have not I
commanded thee? Be strong and of a good courage; be
not afraid, neither be thou dismayed: for the LORD thy
God is with thee whithersoever thou goest.

Have you ever waited for something a long time? Sure, we all have! So, It's important for us to try and remember the emotions that surrounded those "waiting times," so let me give you a few reminders to help you re-create that feeling in your mind.

How about this one: Do you remember when you were in the drive through and you waited and waited and waited for someone to come over the intercom and take your order? If you're like me, the time seemed to slow to almost a standstill between the intercom and the cashier's window and then finally the takeout window!

In the setting of the chapter it's time for Israel to move from the wilderness and move forward into the promise land of Canaan. It's been a long time coming and now the waiting is over. It's time for the promised blessing to be fulfilled.

Here we zoom into the life of Joshua under God's spiritual microscope. Here is the servant of Moses. He had been where Moses had been, done what Moses has done; and carefully watched the leadership of Moses during his many years. Moses had been the leader; Joshua had been the servant and now Moses was dead. There was no opportunity to send Moses a get well card. No time celebrate Moses' death and speak encouraging words; nor time to bring flowers to place upon his grave although it couldn't be found. In fact, God took Moses' body and buried him so no one would make a shrine out of him.

The Israelites thought surely that Moses would be the one who would lead them into the Promised Land. But, Moses was now dead at 102 years of age because of his disobedience in striking the rock in Meribah. He did not glorify God and therefore could not go into the Promised Land. Here are Moses' people witnessing their powerful leader's death. They have a long road ahead of them in confronting a daunting task of crossing the Jordan and conquering Jericho. And Joshua rises up amongst the people to announce, "I'm next in line."

Even when God's powerful, proficient and prestigious leaders pass on. God continues with his plans—God always has someone he can use to accomplish his purposes. Since we do not know or understand who God will choose to use today, each of God's servants should always consider himself to be "in training" for God's use.

I. Joshua's Faithful Obedience:

God raised Joshua as Moses' successor because he learned from Moses and supported Moses as his right-hand man. Joshua obeyed Moses as his faithful assistant. More than anything else, he was a man of faith who supported Moses fully. Joshua was under the shadow of Moses for the last 40 years and now as a gray-haired general he was ready to step into his new role as a leader of the Canaan conquest. I can honestly admit that leaders are not born but are raised up with training and learning.

Joshua under the supervision of Moses had to learn humility; and faithfulness as a servant before God could use him as a leader. The principle is still the same—humble submission to authority always precedes delegated authority in God's service (James 4:10).

Moses was spiritually attracted to Joshua leadership qualities because of his attitude. It's imperative to remember that 90% of your attitudes will determine 10% of favor; which in turn will determine 100% of your next destination.

We all must have the characteristics of Joshua to be a person of commitment: Because of the lack of commitment, marriage fails, students drop out of school, and many forsake the Lord.

II. Joshua's Fastened Observance:

Joshua never took his eyes off Moses' ministry. He never took his eyes off the people and his destiny. He understood how things went disappointingly for Moses when he first began to walk in his destiny as the one who would deliver Israel from Egyptian slavery. You remember! Moses went to Pharaoh and informed him to let Israel go. But Pharaoh did not listen to him.

The people who had recognized him as a leader began to curse him because Pharaoh increased their workload. Moses in his leadership position, successfully led them out of Egypt; and the people complained and muttered and turned against Moses every time something went wrong. Just days after Moses lead the people out of Egypt an army chased them. Shortly after the great deliverance from those soldiers at the Red Sea; the water supply ran out and the people were ready to riot and go back to Egypt. Then the food supply ran out!

Just like Moses! Joshua observed that you will run into all sorts of problems and roadblocks as you walk into your destiny. Don't be surprised when that happens because it is part of the process. Don't panic. God will empower you to overcome each difficulty or problem.

You must not interpret problems or setbacks as an indication to give up and quit. Understand that the devil is going to oppose you and things won't always go smoothly. That is a part of the process. Don't let it throw you when it happens.

Don't quit because of closed doors either. At times you will have to press in to serve God in your calling. You may have to march up to a few closed doors and knock on them. But as you follow God, He will open the doors for you and give you many opportunities to serve Him.

III. Joshua's Factual Obligation:

Joshua was a new leader but there was no sign of fear in his heart. He began to obey God's command right away. He did not delay God's command. Joshua knew God's plan and carried out the task God gave him immediately. He took God's command very seriously. He should have formed an inaugural committee to celebrate his new leadership. But he cared about God more than his own political ambition.

God imparted a leadership gifting into him. The people recognized him as a leader and they stated that they were willing to follow him. This was alarming! Why? The Israelites had a bad track record in heeding Moses leadership. When Moses was alive they opposed his leadership, they whined and complained anytime things did not go perfectly, and they rebelled against God multiple times.

I think that is why God did something supernatural to firmly establish Joshua as a God-appointed leader in the peoples' eyes. God said, in (Joshua 3:7), "*And the LORD said unto Joshua, This day will I begin to magnify thee in the sight of all Israel, that they may know that, as I was with Moses, so I will be with thee.*" Then God had Joshua do the same miracle that Moses had done. Moses parted the Red Sea and let the people cross over on dry land. Joshua parted the Jordan River and the people also crossed over on dry land. You can read all about that in (Joshua chapter 3).

So often we are faced with challenges as we try to move from one thing to something new, and I wonder how many times we give up, and go back, not persevering, and miss out on not only learning something new about ourselves, or about God or about our faith in Him, but miss out on something totally amazing at the other side of the challenge?

Crossings are part of the journey each of us takes to grow to be more and more like Jesus. After all, God didn't save us to make us statues and put us on display in a museum. He saved us to remake us into the image of His Son. He saved us to mature us and equip us to do His will. He saved us to teach us how to be His flesh in this world. I mean, there is more to this Christianity than being delivered from the bondage of sin. So, like the delivered Israelites, each of us has a rich inheritance to cross over and claim our blessing. We must look back before crossing over. So that we can see that God has always helped us make the crossings in the past.

No matter what God calls us to, He establishes us firmly in it. He usually confirms our calling as we start to function in our destiny. Some people phrase it this way: "The anointing makes a way for you." In other words, as people see you operate successfully in your gifted calling, they come into agreement with your calling. As they see God's power and anointing flow through you in your area of ministry. They recognize the call of God on your life.

God desires to open doors for you as you serve him. He will make a way for you to operate in what he has called you to do. He will establish you and provide opportunity for you to do what He has tasked you to do.

Chapter 16

⌒𝓂⌒

The Power of a Prayer Meeting

(Acts 12:5 KJV)
*Peter therefore was kept in prison: but prayer was made
without ceasing of the church unto God for him.*

For centuries the prayer meeting was a central part of church life, an indispensable part of the weekly program. Yet today few churches have a prayer meeting. If you're too busy to pray then you're busier than God wants you to be. There's nothing beyond the reach of prayer except that which is outside the will of God.

What was once a major emphasis of church activities; has been kicked to the sidelines and ignored by most members. Furthermore many prayer meetings today involve little prayer. Even in meetings set aside for prayer, other activities typically crowd in leaving little time for adoration, confession, intercession and thanksgiving to the Lord. But! The Saint Peter Baptist Church knew the power of an effective prayer meeting.

There are times when the dark clouds of evil surround the Church and the future looks dark and dreary. That is how it must have appeared that day when Peter was arrested. James the apostle has recently been murdered by Herod Agrippa I. The crowd loved it, and it seemed the same fate awaited Peter. God watched and noted what Herod was doing to his people.

This evil man was the grandson of Herod the Great, who ordered the massacre of children at Bethlehem. He was the nephew of Herod Antipas who murdered John the Baptist. The Herod family was a devious ruthless family. They were despised by the Jews. They were from the tribe of the Edomites from the south east region of Palestine.

Herod Agrippa I began persecuting the church in an attempt to win favour with the Jews. The Orthodox Jews relentlessly despised those who were called Christians. In those days he began by arresting believers, and even beheaded James. Pleased at his growing popularity, he seized Peter with the same intention to execute him.

Peter is now in prison awaiting execution. He is heavily guarded by sixteen soldiers, four at a time, chained to two guards, with two more watching the doors. Although Herod appeared in masterful control, Peter had something greater. Peter had the Saint Peter Baptist Church, praying for him in a prayer meeting.

We need to pray earnestly for God's divine intervention into the affairs of men. There are many examples of God's divine intervention in Scripture, as a direct result of prayer:

- Moses prayed and God spared Israel from judgment;
- Joshua prayed and God caused the sun to stand still;
- Hannah prayed and God gave her a baby boy;
- Solomon prayed and God gave him wisdom;
- Elijah prayed and God sent fire down from heaven;
- Jonah prayed and God brought him out of the belly of the whale;
- Peter prayed and God raised Dorcas from the dead;
- Paul and Silas prayed until the jail house rocked open;
- The thief on the cross prayed and God gave him eternal life;
- These Christians prayed and God set Peter free from prison.

"Prayer Changes Things"

Scripture is replete with examples of Jesus, Himself, who earnestly prayed:

"And straightway Jesus constrained his disciples to get into a ship, and to go before him unto the other side, while he sent the multitudes away. And when he had sent the multitudes away, he went up into a mountain apart to pray: and when the evening was come, he was there alone" (Matthew 14:22-23).

It was Max Lucado who in his new book titled "Turn," said this about Jesus' prayer life, "Rather than ascend the throne of power, He climbed the mountain of prayer. He went up on a mountainside by Himself to pray." He goes on to say, "Why place such a premium on prayer? When we work, we work. But when we pray, God works. Scripture attaches breathtaking power to prayer."

I have discovered that God rescues, releases, and restores His servants when we pray. I'm reminded of Lazarus, a servant of the Lord, and close friend of Jesus. Lazarus after being dead for four days, the bible says, *"And he that was dead came forth, bound hand and foot with graveclothes: and his face was bound about with a napkin. Jesus saith unto them, Loose him, and let him go"* (John 11:44). If Jesus can raise someone from the dead, and He has, He is quite capable of rescuing and releasing His servants from whatever it is that's holding, binding, or enslaving them.

What is it that you need to be released from? A bad habit? An addiction? A secret sin? If any of these, or anything else, has enslaved you, then hear these words of the Psalmist, *"And call upon me in the day of trouble: I will deliver thee, and thou shalt glorify me"* (Psalm 50:15).

Are you waiting expectantly for God to answer your prayers? Will you be surprised when He does?

I. The Aforementioned Crisis:

Jesus often said persecution will be evident:

"These things I have spoken unto you, that in me ye might have peace. In the world ye shall have tribulation: but be of good cheer; I have overcome the world" (John 16:33).

The people, who were being persecuted, were praying at John Mark's mother's house for Peter. They prayed at one place and God answered at another place. It's always amazed me how Christians can pray for something or someone that is somewhere else and expects an answer, but they don't expect an answer when they pray for things at home.

They understood the power of a prayer meeting:

- It wasn't time to quit praying;
- It wasn't time to run and hide from prayer;
- It wasn't time to disband the church because of prayer not being answered;
- It wasn't time to fire the preacher and hire a diplomat to initiate prayer;
- It was time to pray in unity!

II. The Astonishing Conclusion:

The church prayed for Peter, that an angel entered the prison; and gives Peter a good shake to wake him up. Peter thought it was all a dream, until he discovered himself outside the prison, fully clothed! My friend I'm convinced that, "Prayer Changes Things."

These Church folks prayed for so mightily for Peter off in prison. But! They were shocked and amazed when he actually showed up at the door. The young damsel Rhoda runs and tells the congregation, "Peter is at the door knocking" and they denied her legitimate claim.

Rhoda couldn't believe her eyes. The rest of them couldn't believe their ears. Peter had a harder time getting into the church than out of prison. These Christians in Jerusalem believed God could answer their prayers.

That is why they were praying through the night, but when the answer came to their door, they couldn't believe it. Isn't that so true of us?

We pray for the Whitehouse, and we believe God will move among the political parties to work in Bi-Partisanship. We pray for the World, and we believe God moves all over the Universe. We pray for those who are in the hospitals and we believe that God will move as a Healer. But, many of us are afraid to pray that God will move right now. All you need is the faith of a grain of a mustard seed to move mountains (see Matthew 17:20).

When the Church experiences problems, a prayer meeting will bring you through the storm. You better plan on having some prayer meetings, because problems are bound to come. We need to learn and understand that God rescues and releases His saints for continued Christian service. Hear Peter's own testimony following his rescue from prison.

When Peter came to himself, he said, *"Now I know of a surety, that the LORD hath sent his angel, and hath delivered me out of the hand of Herod, and from all the expectation of the people of the Jews"* (Acts 12:11).

We must face the fact that even in the most fervent prayer meetings there is sometimes a spirit of doubt and unbelief. Whether God takes the storms away when we pray, or more usually calms our hearts in the midst of the storms, we can know with absolute certainty that nothing will happen to us outside His sovereign power or His fatherly love. For God sees our trials. God hears our prayers.

Chapter 17

⌒⁂⌒

Let Go and Let God

(Psalms 3:1-8 KJV)

Lord, how are they increased that trouble me! many are they that rise up against me. Many there be which say of my soul, There is no help for him in God. Selah. But thou, O LORD, art a shield for me; my glory, and the lifter up of mine head. I cried unto the LORD with my voice, and he heard me out of his holy hill. Selah. I laid me down and slept; I awaked; for the LORD sustained me. I will not be afraid of ten thousands of people, that have set themselves against me round about. Arise, O LORD; save me, O my God: for thou hast smitten all mine enemies upon the cheek bone; thou hast broken the teeth of the ungodly. Salvation belongeth unto the LORD: thy blessing is upon thy people. Selah.

You can almost feel a sense of panic as this psalm starts. You can hear the exhaling and inhaling of breathes of anxiety as his chest rises and falls. The person in whom we speak of is David; a man after God's own tender heart. Whichever way he turns there seems to be a multitude of enemies pressing in ready to attack him. The enemy is not only numerous but constantly multiplying against him. The enemy is rising up against David to confront him in order to strike him down. In addition, his adversaries are saying that deliverance or help will not intervene to deliver him this time.

We all face times of trouble, turbulence and turmoil. It is part of our human condition that things don't always go the way we want them to go. It is important to remember that a person is not defined by the amount of trouble they have experienced in their life. Rather, a person is defined by how they respond to that trouble. Do we meet difficulties with faith or with despair? Do we place our trust in God or abandon all hope? Do we respond to circumstances with calm assurance or with agonizing worry? David made a choice how he would respond to his conflict.

David was one of many people in the bible who had more than his share of trouble:

- He was pursued by King Saul;
- He barely escaped several assassination attempts;
- He had to spend much time hiding in the wilderness;
- His entire family was taken captive;
- His friends revolted against him and were ready to kill him;
- He suffered the shame of having committed adultery and murder;
- His son Amnon raped his daughter Tamar;
- His other son Absalom murdered Amnon;
- Absalom led a revolt against him as father;
- Absalom himself whom he loved was killed, much to David's grief.

David was certainly a man with many problems. Yet somehow, he survived them all and has come to be remembered as "a man after God's own heart." How was he able to do this? Answer! He had the Lord on his side.

I. David's Expressible Discovery:

The penning of this particular Psalm occurred during a time when David fled from his son Absalom. It seems according to (2 Samuel 15:1-16), that Absalom knew David intended Solomon to be heir of the throne. So Absalom conspired to gain the favor of the people, and deliberately devised a plan to execute his father. He obtained derogatory advice to rebel against David from Ahithophel. Ahithophel was a counselor of King David and a man greatly renowned for his sagacity. At the time of Absalom's revolt he deserted David and espoused the cause of Absalom to kill his father.

In result to Absalom's rebellion; David and his court had to flee for safety while they organized a counter attack. As David left Jerusalem and the surrounding towns, some of the people cried, some pledged support, but others decried his rule and taunted him. It is human nature for us to be hurt the most by those who come against us.

It seemed apparent, that most of Israel loved and supported David, but all he could think about was those who conspired against him. This must have been a difficult time since the pain came from his family members. Believe it or not we are hurt mostly by those whom we care about the most.

If you have been betrayed or feeling like the whole world is against you; I pray that you have the confidence that comes from turning to the Lord, so that you won't suffocate yourselves in fear of men. Perhaps you are filled with anxiety, give your concerns to the Lord in prayer and lay your head down for a peaceful rest. Perhaps your head is down; depressed or saddened. The Lord is a lifter! The Lord will lift your head up. The Lord is placing His hand under some of your chins even right now and pulling you out of your misery. Keep your head up, and set your eyes on the Lord who gives you strength. It does not matter where you are in your life. It only matters where God is going to take you. I decree that every stone, that man has ever thrown to knock you down. It will be used as a stepping stone to lift you up.

II. David's Expedient Departure:

The pain of betrayal can be so strong that you find it hard to sleep. Well, David was overthrown and ran out of Jerusalem by his own son Absalom. In my mind, I am picturing a tired man; who is sleepless and paranoid.

David didn't fight back. Instead of playing defense he rallied his family, bodyguards and assistants and left Jerusalem to go into hiding. Instead of fighting back at Absalom; David was able to save lives, avoid civil war and most importantly he allowed God to fight the battle for him.

Zadok and a company of priests and Levites left with David carrying the Ark of the Covenant with them. The Ark represented the presence and also the government of God. It was the centerpiece of Israel's life and worship. The Ark leaving symbolized God Himself leaving Jerusalem. Without it Jerusalem's sacrifice would be in vain. So, rather than moving the Ark, David sent the priests back with the ark in the faith that if God was for him, and would return back to Jerusalem. This taught me that you shouldn't stop praising God just because someone is against you or your protocol. Neither should you do things to cut off other people's blessings and ability to worship God.

As David fled into the wilderness he had to climb the Mount of Olives barefooted. He dwelled in the mountain in order to keep an eye on the Ark of the Covenant. While at the foot of the Mountain he begins to ask God to turn the council of Ahithophel into foolishness. When David reached the top of the Mountain, God had sent him a helper to answer his prayer and confound the council of Ahithophel. Ahithophel, after sowing his advice of venomous discourse; he hanged himself (2 Samuel 17:23). Which symbolizes that God will hang the head of our enemies and render us victorious. He hears when His children call out to Him in need and answers our prayers.

"Ask and it shall be given, seek and you shall find, knock and the door shall be opened."
(Matthew 7:7)

III. David's Excellent Delectation:

Although David, was humiliated and betrayed by his first born Absalom. David always treated Absalom as a son. He never issued an executive order to any of his men to kill Absalom, only to bring him back alive. We would do well to learn not to kill our enemies when we have the upper hand against them. We are to treat them as we would our own son and daughter with mercy.

David was threatened to lose his kingdom, his wealth, he even was threatened to lose his life. I think he had plenty of stresses to keep him sleepless, don't you? Yet what did he say? Read verse 5, "*I laid me down and slept; I awaked; for the LORD sustained me*". David enjoyed the peace and patience of God.

David talks about how he was able to sleep because God was helping him. He even says that he won't be afraid of "many thousands of people". Where did David get such fearlessness? The answer is in verse 3 where David calls the Lord a "*shield about me*", "*my glory*", and "*the lifter of my head*".

Despite Absalom's impressive line-up of all Israel and the leaders of Judah, God was against him for his acts of rebellion. The most famous scenes in the bible is the episode of the mule riding Absalom getting his Nazarene's long hair hopelessly entangled in the branches of a great tree, leaving him "suspended between heaven and earth as the mule passed on from under him"(2nd Samuel 18:1-18). The very hair about which Absalom had been so vain now proved to be his undoing!

Remember, friends and family will turn on you, and leave you out in the desert to die; but God will resurrect you. God loves us so, just as he loved David. Whenever you need Him, don't be afraid to petition Him. God will beckon our call and answer our prayers.

Chapter 18

⁓

Get Up It's Over

(John 5:8 KJV)
Jesus saith unto him, Rise, take up thy bed, and walk.

The scene in its tenor and tone introduced to us in this passage is indeed a sight of sympathetic sadness and sorrowfulness. The background is the pool of Bethesda in Jerusalem, around which lay a great multitude of incapable individuals. The great Physician approaches this crowd of sufferers, who were not only sick but self-reliant lying around upon five porches. But there was no more stir among them than in the quiet waters of the pool. When the great Physician arrives He was neither wanted nor recognized. Addressing one of the most helpless of the sufferers; the Lord look at his condition and asked him if he is desirous of being made whole.

Instead of responding to Jesus with a prompt request that He would have mercy upon him; this man thought only of the pool and of some man to assist him into the chilly choppy waters. In the light of what has been said, how exceedingly significant and blessed to note that we are told the pool which was called Bethesda, meaning "mercy" was by the "sheep" gate. It is only in Christ that the poor sinner can find mercy, and it is only through His sacrifice on the Cross that this mercy is now obtainable for us in Him.

I. The Subliminal concern of Christ:

It's a divine pleasure in our finite frailty to notice carefully every single word of God. There is nothing insignificant in the word of God. The least detail has a meaning and value; every name, every geographical and topographical reference has value. In fact, the subliminal concern of Christ in this text is His grace, favor and His mercy.

As I inspect the interception of verse 2, notice the last words of the verse *"having five porches" Now there is at Jerusalem by the sheep market a pool, which is called in the Hebrew tongue Bethesda, having five porches* (John 5:2). Let us note that biblical numerology is significant in this verse.

The Bible seems to use biblical numerology in patterns or to teach a spiritual truth:

For Example: The number of the porches here is momentous. In Scripture the numerals are used with Divine design and precision:

Five stands for *grace, favor or mercy*: It was with five loaves the Lord Jesus fed the hungry multitude. The fifth clause in the Lord's Prayer is, "Give us this day our daily bread." The fifth Commandment was the only one with a promise attached to it. Thus we see the perfect propriety of *five* porches around the pool of Bethesda in its meaning called *mercy*, situated "by the *sheep* gate."

There's a great number of impotent, blind, halt, and withered waited upon the porches and watched for the moving of the water in the pool of Bethesda.

- The impotent—They are feeble and deficient in vigour, authority, force, and efficiency. They are classified as inadequate and inferior in their spiritual lives. They are no use for society or the Kingdom of God.
- The blind—Their spiritual awareness is obscured and hazy. Spiritual matters are vague, ambiguous, and unknown to them.

They are in the worldly dark and have no concept of the spiritual light. *"They have a form of Godliness"* (2 Timothy 3:5).

- The halt—People who are lame, and unable to stand erectly, and move toward the Lord God. They are unable to walk a straight path, and have great difficulty understanding the things of God.
- The withered—Dry and barren of the influence and Spirit of God, resulting in a lack of vitality and regeneration of their spiritual lives.

Jesus is determined to look pass their conditions and extend living hope, not only to their physical stability, but their souls as well. These four individuals represent darkness, but Jesus represents the light that leads them out of darkness.

II. The Skepticism of the Communities:

Assuming the explanation in (John 5:4) is accurate, everyone gathered together, and waited at the pool of Bethesda, for an angel to stir the water so they could be healed.

"For an angel went down at a certain season into the pool, and troubled the water: whosoever then first after the troubling of the water stepped in was made whole of whatsoever disease he had" (John 5:4).

Here's something interesting to think about, *"miraculous healings"* at the pool of Bethesda are not like any other healing I find in the Bible. Think about it. Have you ever read of any such miracle in the Bible, where an angel somehow energizes the waters, and the first person into the water is healed? Where do we ever read of angels being involved with healings? Water is often used in healings, but such miracles are always specific—not general. Naaman was healed of his leprosy when he obeyed Elisha's instructions to dip himself seven times in the muddy Jordan River (2 Kings 5). People are healed individually and specifically, not in some kind of "whoever can get there first" manner. There is something very bizarre, very unusual about this "miracle." Does God really heal someone because he can push and shove and bully his way into the pool first? No!

I think it's important for us to recognize that some people focus more on superstition, rather than focusing on the supernatural. Here is a man who was looking to the water for his healing, that's called superstition. In order to get his blessing, he must take his eyes off of the water and look to Jesus the supernaturalists.

If we are looking to other things for our healing or deliverance, let us turn our eyes toward Jesus. The man could not be healed until he looked to Jesus. But wait one minute! I commend this man because he didn't have a waiting problem!

For thirty-eight long years this man laid upon his pallet beside the pool of Bethesda, but he waited. He couldn't walk, but he waited. There were no wheelchairs around, but he waited. The pool was not ADA compliant, but he waited.

Most of our congregation isn't thirty-eight years old, and we wonder if things will ever change. Be encouraged! Don't get in a hurry keep on waiting! Thirty-eight years is a long time to wait for anything. If you haven't suffered for at least 38 years, thank God for his grace, favor and mercy.

This man no matter what it took, he stayed his course. He has only the mercy of others at his hands. His friends and family members, who carried him to the Bethesda pool in the morning, and pick him up at evening, left him by himself. They are nowhere to be found to help slide him into the pool for his healing in which he believed existed. Day after day, year after year, he continues to share stories with those who suffer alongside hoping to win the angelic healing lottery one day. But be confident! What God has for you is for you. Don't worry a change is going to come.

This impotent man lucky day arrived. The Son of God enters into his jail cell of dependency and asks, *"Wilt thou be made whole?"* Listen, God doesn't ask us questions because he lacks information. The question is a gift to lead our thoughts and mind in the right direction. Possibly the healing brings with it a price that should be considered. Let's try to unpack this question by asking it in a different way.

Do you want to leave all of your dependencies? Do you want to work all day? Do you want to leave behind all excuses and take on the full responsibility of life? Many of our desperate prayers to God have a price in their answer. This Scripture can apply not only to those with physical disabilities, but all of our emotional and spiritual ones as well.

Jesus asks us all, "Wilt thou be made whole?" Do you really want the new and harder job, or is it more convenient to complain about money? Do you want to leave loneliness behind, and take on the joy and responsibility of a relationship with a person who will heal the isolation, but also force us to altar our selfish lifestyle?

Jesus asked the man an intriguing question? "Do you want to get well?" Of course this man does! "Why would he be there if he didn't want to get well?" Is it possible Jesus knew something we don't? In the response to Jesus' question, the man starts with excuses.

"The impotent man answered him, Sir, I have no man, when the water is troubled, to put me into the pool: but while I am coming, another steppeth down before me" (John 5:7).

Let me hurriedly express to each of you, "God has some right now blessings, but we have to get rid of our later on intentions." You want divine deliverance but not right now. You want to posses that agape love but not right now, you have some more folks on the hit list to put out of business. You want be happy, but not willing to change your inconsistent lifestyle. Right now!

We all know of people who profess to want help out of their circumstance, but really want help to stay in it. I call them the "will work for food" people. They are sitting at heavy traffic areas with a dog, with a hand-printed cardboard sign that says "will work for food." When you offer work for them, they refuse the offer to work by promoting their disability. Here's my conclusion for these individuals, "they don't want to work for food." As long as people continued to toss money to them for just sitting there, with a pity party face. Get up and do something about your situation.

III. The Saviors' Conclusion

"Jesus *saith unto him, Rise, take up thy bed, and walk. And immediately the man was made whole, and took up his bed, and walked: and on the same day was the sabbath*" (John 5:8-9).

Jesus Christ told the man "Rise, take up thy bed, and walk." Get Up It's Over!

The impotent man received healing through the words of Jesus Christ. The Living Water of God, His flowing grace of redemption and restoration, was embodied by the person of His Son, Jesus Christ. Jesus had the authority and the power of his Father to bestow healing and make whole!

1) **Rise**—Wake up and stand up. Don't sit or lie down and wait for your disease to bring you to death through obscurity and inactivity in your natural life. Stand upon your feet like a strong, spiritual man made whole!

2) **Take up thy bed**—Expiate your sin by making amends. Reject the dirty sin that made you sick and put you into that bed. Extinguish your guilt of sin. Go and sin no more.

3) **Walk**—Live, Live, Live. You are made whole and alive. Move forward and walk toward your Saviour and your God.

When we ask God for healing in any area of our lives, we are really asking for bigger problems to solve. Let's ask God to challenge us, to help us to take up our mats, burn our bridges of dependency and walk forward solving greater and greater problems for as many people as He allows, for as long as He allows. Get up it's over!

Chapter 19

Check Yourself; Before You
Wreck Yourself

(Matthew 7:1-5 KJV)
Judge not, that ye be not judged. For with what
judgment ye judge, ye shall be judged: and with what
measure ye mete, it shall be measured to you again. And
why beholdest thou the mote that is in thy brother's eye,
but considerest not the beam that is in thine own eye?
Or how wilt thou say to thy brother, Let me pull out the
mote out of thine eye; and, behold, a beam is in thine
own eye? Thou hypocrite, first cast out the beam out of
thine own eye; and then shalt thou see clearly to cast out
the mote out of thy brother's eye.

An old man was sitting out on his front porch whitlin' and enjoying
the sunny day. Into town drove a stranger who stopped in front
of the old man's house. The stranger rolled down his car window,
stuck his head out and yelled, "Hey, old man, what kind of people are in
this town?"

The old gent leaned back, looked at the stranger and said, "Well fella,
just what kind of people were there in the town you just came from?"

"Why they were the most unfriendly, unlikable and disagreeable folks you ever saw" the man replied.

"Well," answered the old man, "That's just the kind of people that are in this town." With that answer the stranger roared off out of town and out of sight. A little while later, into town drove another stranger. This man saw the older man on his porch and he pulled up, stopped the car and got out.

"Good afternoon sir. How are you this fine day?" the young man cheerfully called out.

"I'm doin' very well thank you and it is a mighty fine day" the older man grinned.

"Well sir, I'm a little new around here, mind if I sit and we talk a bit?" the younger man inquired.

"Sure, come on up here and sit" the older man invited.

The younger man ambled up and took a seat on the broad porch.

"Well, there is really just one question I have," he began, "What kind of people are in this town?"

The older man gently smiled, "Well, just what kind of people were in the town you came from?"

"Well sir, they were the friendliest, nicest, most likable folks you'd ever want to meet" the young man eagerly responded.

"Well, my good friend, that's jus' the kind of folks you'll find here."

Author Unknown

I. The Attitude of Unfriendly People:

What kind of people are in this congregation? Psychologists have recognized a fundamental principle in human relations to this specific subject matter. People tend to criticize in others the very things they dislike about themselves.

If someone feels bad about themselves, they can notice something bad about you and point it out, and they feel more equal to you, which brings them up a little. Or they are simply down or out of control and it bring you down because you allow them to.

The first thing to know is that a happy, self confident, person does not put others down. They might provide constructive criticism but they won't put others down. This tells you a lot about the person who criticizes you.

Some people are extremely negative about others because:

- They need to make themselves feel like they're in control or more powerful or to cover up their own insecurities.
- They've experienced a trauma of their own in the past and they don't know how to deal with the pain so they'll hurt others as a defense mechanism.
- The Bible recognizes this behavior of self-deception. It is the problem of trying to hide one's own faults by criticizing another. Jesus warned about those who look for specks in others, while they carry a plank in their own eye (Matthew 7:1-5). Emotionally detaching from a person like this can be hard to do but you need to refuse to become involved. That person wants you to feel badly about yourself. Don't give them that power!

I saw a button once that said, "If you can't say something nice about someone, sit next to me so I can hear you better." We're all guilty of speaking negatively of others! Jesus' command is a call to stop gossiping about one another, or slandering one another. We're not to paste someone's faults upon a billboard for others for review and critique and evaluate one another.

II. The Anticipation of Removing the Plank:

Have you ever complained that a congregation or another Christian was unfriendly? Maybe they were not friendly or maybe they were. Instead of complaining how unfriendly others are to me, I need to seriously ask the Lord and myself, "Lord, is it I?" (Matthew 22:26).

Am I the one who turns and looks the other way to keep from speaking to someone? Am I the one who quickly slips into a tight-circle of family or friends and ignore others? Am I the one who races for the door the minute services are over? Am I the one who refuses to speak unless the other person speaks first? When I accuse another of being unfriendly, am I being unfriendly?

Jesus told speck seekers, "You hypocrite, first take the plank out of your own eye, and then you will see clearly to remove the speck from your brother's eye" (Matthew 7:5).

III. The Antidotes to Being Friendly:

The wise man of Proverbs provided a solution on how to handle those we think are unfriendly! "A man that hath friends must shew himself friendly" (Proverbs 18:24).

If you think someone is unfriendly to you, then you need to become friendlier. Maybe the person you think is unfriendly is just shy. Maybe they are waiting for you to speak first. Maybe they are thinking about other things. Maybe they have troubles and burdens that are bothering them.

"Many will entreat the favour of the prince: and every man is a friend to him that giveth gifts" (Proverbs 19:6). If you want others to be your friends and friendly to you, you must be generous, loving and giving to them.

Those who see all others as unfriendly are unwilling to give what it takes to receive friendliness. Receivers of friendliness are givers of warm smiles, hearty handshakes and kind encouraging words.

Don't wait for the other person to approach and talk to you, walk up and talk to them. Smile and be friendly. You'll be amazed how friendly people, who you thought were unfriendly, can be.

IV. The Affections of the Friendliest, Nicest, Most Likable Folks:

Before I complain about other people, I need to see if I am part of the problem. If the congregation is unfriendly then it is up to me to be friendly and to change the protocol. Then I can say, "This congregation has the friendliest, nicest, most likeable folks you'd ever want to meet!"

Chapter 20

⟨↲⟩

The Resurrected Redeemer

(Matthew 28:6 KJV)
He is not here: for he is risen, as he said. Come, see the
place where the Lord lay.

In this chapter Matthew tells us about "an angel of the Lord." The last time we have seen an angel of the Lord in Matthew's Gospel is in the story of Christ's birth. At Christ's birth the angel was a messenger from the Lord; he explained to Joseph the meaning of Mary's pregnancy and gave him precise instructions from God; to take Mary home as his wife. We immediately see that this angel too is a messenger from the Lord and he explains the meaning of the empty tomb and gives instructions from God Himself to the women at the tomb. *"He is not here: for he is risen, as he said. Come, see the place where the Lord lay" (Matthew 28:6).*

The resurrection of Jesus Christ has very important meaning. It was the final proof that everything He had said was true. He has endured His betrayal by Judas, an arrest in the garden of Gethsemane, an unjustified trial before Pontius Pilate, a horrendous beating with a torching whip, and a hammering down of His body by nails to a wooden cross. But that's not the end of the story, "And He died!" The synoptic gospels declared that His body was buried namely by Nicodemus, and Joseph of Arimathea both of whom were His secret disciples. It's no doubt after His burial that He rose after such gruesome crucifixion from physical death back to a literal to life with an unidentified body and then ascended to heaven.

In dealing with the death of Jesus; Satan got a thrill out of such horrific suffering. But the great thrill of the crucifixion is not the fact Jesus died, many have died. The thrill is the fact Jesus died, and now lives. The good news from the grave yard declares that Jesus rose and left the dead, and caused Satan's empire to crumble. There will never be a tomb compared to Jesus' tomb. The tomb of Buddha has a body in it. The tomb of Mohammed has a body in it. But the tomb of Jesus is empty. Hallelujah!

I. Because of His Resurrection We Have a Pardon:

Jesus Christ came into this world to die as our substitute for our sins. The sinless Son of God came to give His life as a ransom for many (Matthew 20:28). While Jesus was alive, He had predicted that He would rise from the dead. He challenged his enemies, *"Destroy this temple, and in three days I will raise it up."* He was speaking about his bodily resurrection (John 2:19). Jesus also told His disciples many times that He would be killed by the leaders in Jerusalem which were welded in Judaism, but be raised to life on the third day. The leaders who killed Jesus were aware of this prediction that He would rise from the dead. Although they did not believe it, they wanted to ensure that it would not happen, so they set a guard around the tomb.

Now the next day, that followed the day of the preparation, the chief priests and Pharisees came together unto Pilate, Saying, Sir, we remember that that deceiver said, while he was yet alive, After three days I will rise again. Command therefore that the sepulchre be made sure until the third day, lest his disciples come by night, and steal him away, and say unto the people, He is risen from the dead: so the last error shall be worse than the first. Pilate said unto them, Ye have a watch: go your way, make it as sure as ye can. So they went, and made the sepulchre sure, sealing the stone, and setting a watch (Matthew 27:62-66).

But the strategy of the Chief Priests and Pharisees didn't succeed? Despite their scheme, Jesus rose from the dead a conqueror. Remember how Jesus had said to Martha, "I am the resurrection and the life?" During

His ministry on earth, Jesus brought a number of people to life from the dead, including Martha's brother Lazarus, who had been dead for four days (John 11). But the resurrection of Jesus Christ was different. It was not just resuscitation, as was the case with Lazarus, who later died again. On the third day Jesus was raised from the dead with a transformed body that was clothed with immortality and glory. His resurrection body could appear and disappear, go through material objects, and ascend to and descend from heaven.

Therefore, after appearing to God as the ultimate sacrifice; Jesus signed my pardon with His blood! I was guilty of my impurities and now the judge became my defense attorney.

II. Because of His Resurrection We have a Promise:

Jesus said unto her, I am the resurrection, and the life: he that believeth in me, though he were dead, yet shall he live (John 11:25).

To see the vacant cross, and to look at an empty tomb gives us the promise of everlasting life byway of Jesus! As I tried to get a handle on the excitement of this particular day, I thought of Mary, the mother of Jesus. I tried to imagine what it was like for her when she heard of her Son's resurrection. She had witnessed her Son's death. She had gone to her new home with the apostle John. But suddenly on the third day she shouted with unspeakable joy, "He has risen!" This news is electrifying! Energizing! It transcends us into life, not in steps, but in leaps! Because of His resurrection we have the promise of eternal life. Despite the oppression of Satan! Jesus was unstoppable.

- Jesus took a tragedy and turned it into a triumph.
- Jesus took the crucifixion and turned it into a commemoration.
- Jesus took darkness and turned it into deliverance.

I wish every believer knew of Him by saying their ABC'S:

A. Ancient of Days, Alpha & Omega, Anchor, Advocate, Author, and the Almighty.

B. Bright Morning Star, Bread of Life, Branch, Bridegroom, Beginning and the End.

C. Christ Jesus, Chief Cornerstone, Champion of Salvation, and the Chief Shepherd.

D. Dayspring From On High, Door to the Sheepfold, and the Deliverer from Darkness.

E. Emmanuel, El Shaddai, Elohim, and the Everlasting Father.

F. Finisher of Our Faith, Friend of Sinners, and the Forerunner of God.

G. Great High Priest, Good Shepherd, God, Great Physician, and the Glory of Israel.

H. Head of the Church, High Tower, Holy One, Hiding Place, and Hope of Glory.

I. I Am that I Am, Image of God, Intercessor, Immortal, and the Invisible.

J. Jesus Christ, Judge, Jehovah-Jireh, Jehovah-Rapha, and Jehovah-Shalom.

K. King of Kings, King of Glory, Kinsman Redeemer, and the Keeper of the Keys.

L. Lord of All, Lamb of God, Light of the World, Lion of Judah, and the Living Water.

M. Messiah, Most High God, Maker, Man of Sorrows, and the Master.

N. Narrow Way, Nebuchadnezzar's Fourth Man in the Fire, and the man from Nazareth.

O. Only Begotten Son, Offering Once and for All, and the Offspring of David.

P. Prince of Peace, Prince of Life, Prophet Like unto Moses, and the Power of God.

Q. Quickener of Transgressors, Quietness and Confidence, and Quieter of Storms.

R. Rose of Sharon, Rock of Salvation, Root of Jesse, and the Resurrection of Life.

S. Son of God, Son of Man, Servant, Savior, Shiloh, Strength, Song, and the Shield.

T. Teacher, True Vine, and the Truth.

U. Unction from the Holy One.

V. Victor, Virgin-Born, Veil-Splitter, and the Vice-Ruler at the Fathers Right Hand.

W. Word of Life, Witness, Wonderful Counselor, Warrior, and Wisdom of God.

X. Xempt from Death Forevermore.

Y. Yoke-Destroyer.

Z. Zacchaeus House Guest.

Now I know my **ABC'S** next time want you say them with me. Jesus has promised us by emptying the grave that, "after this life we all shall live!"

III. Because of His Resurrection We have a Place:

As Christians, we've been given a genuine deed to heaven; the promise of eternal life, an inheritance and a mansion that can never be foreclosed on. Our ownership in Christ is documented in the Word of God, and our names are registered in the Lamb's Book of Life.

But many Christians fear that a thief—the devil—is going to rob them of their title deed. They have little assurance of ownership.

Your heavenly home was bought for a price, and that payment results in a title deed that can never be lost through foreclosure. You can go joyfully into your day's activities and rest peacefully knowing that your salvation is secure and your home in heaven is being prepared for you!

"In my Father's house are many mansions: if it were not so, I would have told you. I go to prepare a place for you. And if I go and prepare a place for you, I will come again, and receive you unto myself; that where I am, there ye may be also" (John 14:2-3).

So, Heaven is real, and it's more like home than any we'll ever know, and when we get there, there'll be no sorrow but only joy and growing in fellowship with Christ and other believers.

Chapter 21

⌒᷍⌒

I May be Down;
but I'm Not Out

(2 Timothy 4:6-7 KJV)
*For I am now ready to be offered, and the time of my
departure is at hand. I have fought a good fight, I have
finished my course, I have kept the faith.*

Let me ask you a few simple questions. Have you ever been
disappointed when things did not go well? Have you been
discouraged to the point of losing hope that things were never
going to change? Have you ever felt defeated in your task and simply
contemplated on quitting?

I remember indistinctly watching the New Orleans Saints back in
2010 playing the Super Bowl. I remember preaching a sermon to the
congregation on that particular Sunday morning called, "God's Super Bowl
Game." I spoke courageously about the Saints and how I was confidant
of them winning.

I remember getting a called from a member of our congregation;
Brother Earnest Bates on my cell. Brother Bates stated, "Pastor, It's
looking mighty bad for those Saints!" I responded by saying, "But the
game isn't over." He was absolutely right! The Saints were looking pitiful.
But surprisely they made a comeback! They were down, but not out. They

never quit trying when faced with disappointment. It was the greatest comeback in NFL history!

Although they were down and things looked hopeless for them; the Saints never saw it that way. They refused to let the discouragement take them out of the game. They were down but never out.

As you move and maneuver in ministry, expect to be knocked down by the Devil, but don't let him take you out. Don't let disappointment and discouragement lead you to defeat.

In (2 Timothy 4) we read how that time had come for Paul. In fewer than one hundred words, he shares with us the hardship of his present, the heartbeat of his past and the hope he holds for the future. In this brief passage Paul reflects on his life and ministry. He looks around, looks back and then he looks ahead. With the finish line in sight, as he picks up the pace, Paul sums up his dynamic life and his hope in death. The lessons we learn from this aging apostle will enable us to run well today, while encouraging us to finish strong tomorrow. In our scriptural reading we see that the Apostle Paul also faced an end—not to a year, but to his life. And like us, as the end is coming, Paul thinks on the past and looks toward the future.

Paul was in prison. He knew there was little chance of his getting out. He knew that he was soon going to die a martyr's death under Nero's chopping block. He says, *"For I am now ready to be offered, and the time of my departure is at hand"* (2 Timothy 4:6). The Greek original language of this text raises the image of a ship. Its anchor has been lifted, its sails have been unfurled, and it is about to depart for distant ports. That's Paul—the time of his departure has almost arrived. His cup is almost empty, and almost all the sands of time allotted to him have run through the hour-glass. So he prepares to pass his baton to his protégée Timothy. He explains to Timothy, "Ministry wouldn't be easy as expected."

The Apostle Paul's ministry brought difficulties, disappointments, and even discouragement, but he never quit; he never let it take him out of the work that God had called him to do. At the end of his life he was able to write.

For I am now ready to be offered, and the time of my departure is at hand. I have fought a good fight, I have finished my course, I have kept the faith (2 Timothy 4:6-7).

Paul knowing that he would soon be executed by Nero. He wrote this final epistle to prepare his successor Timothy; to fulfill and complete his own ministry after the passing of his mentor. Through this letter written to this young preacher; Paul helps prepare us to meet the difficulties, disappointments, and discouragements of ministry as well.

In this letter Paul advised Timothy to expect disappointing and even discouraging situations in the future. They will try to knock him down, but encouraged him, "Don't let them knock you out!"

I. Ministry brings Unrealistic Expectation:

Why would Paul refer to the difficulties of ministry when Timothy needed encouragement? I suggest that unrealistic expectations are often the cause of later discouragement and even defeat. In order to be truly prepared for ministry in the real world; whether on a church staff, as a deacon, as a layperson, or perhaps as a missionary. We must expect ministry to be often difficult and sometimes discouraging.

Understanding the simplicity of ministry is imperative. Ministry is the giving up of everything without expecting anything in return. You don't expect a pat on the back or even a thank you. You do it out of love and for nothing else.

Jesus told us that the first and greatest commandment was to love God our father with all our heart and soul and strength (Mark 12:30). But he then added that the second greatest commandment was to love our neighbors as ourselves and that all the laws and teaching of the prophets hung on these two commandments (Mark 12:31).

Ministry is not a visiting the sick and shut in, although that can be ministry. Ministry is not preaching from a pulpit, but it certainly can be. Ministry is not teaching a Sunday school class, but it can be.

What is ministry then? It is letting God use you for the spreading of His word and permissive will. Supporting the needs of the church can be a ministry if you do it for the Glory of God. Cutting a yard at a needy person's house can be a ministry if you do it for the Glory of God. Are you catching on?

People can visit the sick and the shut in but if their heart is not in the right place it is just action. People preach from pulpits but if their heart is not right it is just words. People can teach Sunday school but if their heart is not in it for God then it is just a lesson. As the Bible says, do all things for the Glory of God and that is ministry. If you approach it with that attitude, then you will reflect the love of God. But! Ministry was never intended to be for show, but it's a sacrifice.

Instead of telling Timothy to be encouraged because his ministry would be a great success, Paul did just the opposite. Paul encouraged Timothy to embrace the same kinds of experiences that he was having:

Be not thou therefore ashamed of the testimony of our Lord, nor of me his prisoner: but be thou partaker of the afflictions of the gospel according to the power of God (2 Timothy 1:8).

II. Ministry brings Unbearable Exhaustion:

What kinds of suffering was Paul calling Timothy to accept and share?

Paul experienced a serious ministry oxymoron. If we had time to discuss the entire book, we would see that Paul was not only dealing with the difficulty of persecution, but he also faced disappointment with believers who let him down. (2 Timothy 1:15) says that everybody in Asia turned away from him. (2 Timothy 4:10) says that Demas deserted him because he loved the present age, and (2 Timothy 4:16) says that all deserted him when he went to court. How discouraging it must have been to look around and see that his co-laborers were no longer there, that his friends were missing in action when the situation became risky and unbearable!

Moreover, Paul warned Timothy about people such as Alexander, Hymaneus, and Philetus who opposed him or strayed from the truth. He forewarned him to stay away from the troublemakers in the church. Ministry was hard; there were people who disappointed him and others who obstructed the work. At the beginning of both chapters 3 and 4 Paul alerted Timothy that things would get even worse in the future. Paul warned him to expect the unraveling of persecution.

Timothy faced many of the same challenges we face today. He faced disappointment with church people, even leaders; lack of support when he needed it; and lack of visible results. Paul over and over essentially said to Timothy, "It may appear hopeless and you may get knocked down but don't be counted out."

All of us gets knocked down every now and then. But you're not in this alone! **Elijah** was down when he was ran out of town by Jezebel, but God lifted him. **Nehemiah** was down after the people tried to stop the rebuilding of the temple, but God lifted him. **Isaiah** was down after his uncle king Uzzah died, but God lifted him. **Ezekiel** was down when he saw the dry bones in the valley, but God lifted him. **Hosea** was down after he married a woman of whoredom, but God lifted him. **Jonah** was down because of the task to preach to Nineveh, but God lifted him. **Peter** was down before he was converted, but God lifted him. If you are down and out, remember that God is a lifter!

How was Timothy to make it through such hard times and not give up?

In (2 Timothy 1:6-7) Paul said, "*Wherefore I put thee in remembrance that thou stir up the gift of God, which is in thee by the putting on of my hands. For God hath not given us the spirit of fear; but of power, and of love, and of a sound mind.*"

Here at the outset of his letter, Paul reminded Timothy of God's gifting and calling. When we face the expected difficulties, disappointments, and discouragements in ministry, we, too, should review our unique missions.

Paul knew His God so well that he expected God to turn any situation, no matter how much it looked like a loss and use it as a victory. That meant that he not only remembered his call and the One who called him, he also entrusted the disappointing or discouraging situation to God, expecting Him to turn it around.

When you face discouragement, do what Paul did, remember your call and know the one who called you. Then, you, too, can entrust your situations to God, knowing His character and promises so that you are down but not out.

III. Ministry brings Unspeakable Enjoyment:

Finally, Paul, knowing that the end is near, he thinks on the past. He doesn't think in terms of financial gain or loss, children, parties, weddings, or funerals. When Paul considers the past he contemplates the state of his soul. When Paul considers the past he looks at how well he has served the Lord. What does Paul say about himself? He says, (2 Timothy 4:7) "*I have fought the good fight, I have finished my course, I have kept the faith.*"

Guarding Paul were Imperial soldiers of the Roman army. It was boring duty. More than once they must have wondered why they were guarding what seemed like a harmless old man. Yet, they guarded him anyway because of the oath they took upon joining the army.

"I have kept the faith," says Paul. Like a good Roman soldier he has been true and obedient. Paul knew first hand of many people who had slipped from the faith. He knew of persons in whom the Gospel flourished for a brief time only to wither and die. He knew of individuals who had left the church and turned or returned to a life of sin. He knew souls that fell into error and heresy. "As for me," says Paul, "I have kept the faith."

Paul has fought the "good" fight. This means he fought to the end. He never quit the struggle. He never gave up. He fought the good fight to the end. "I have finished my course." Again, the emphasis is on the fact that he never quit, that he never gave up, and that he kept on going and fighting and running for the Lord. "I have kept the faith." He didn't fall away. Again, the emphasis is on the fact that he never quit, that he never gave up, and that he kept on going and fighting and running for the Lord.

Chapter 22

⌒✳⌒

The Man Who Carried
Jesus' Cross

(Matthew 27:32 KJV)
And as they came out, they found a man of Cyrene,
Simon by name: him they compelled to bear his cross.

Black History Month is an annual celebration of achievements by Black Americans and a time for recognizing the central role of African Americans in U.S. history. The event grew out of "Negro History Week," the brainchild of noted historian Carter G. Woodson and other prominent African Americans. Since 1976, every U.S. president has officially designated the month of February as Black History Month. Other countries around the world, including Canada and the United Kingdom, also devote a month to celebrating Black History. So, I would like to take a moment to commemorate the African Americans National Heritage.

There's a story often told about Jackie Robinson the first African American to play major league baseball. He faced jeering crowds in every stadium. While playing one day in his home stadium in Brooklyn, he committed an error. The fans began to ridicule him. During a delay in the game Robinson stood at second base, humiliated, his head down and began to sob.

The fans jeered and threw things at him. But about that time, Brooklyn's shortstop Pee Wee Reese, came over and stood next to him. He put his arm around Jackie Robinson and faced the crowd. And as they stood there; the fans grew quiet. Robinson later said, "That arm around my shoulder saved my career." Today I want to look at the story of a man mentioned briefly in the gospels: Simon of Cyrene. He also comes and puts an arm around Jesus.

When my mind ponders upon the thought of Black History; I think of this biblical character named Simon. Simon was a fascinating man. He was a Jewish pilgrim coming into Jerusalem from out of the country. He was a good old fashion countryman, and not a city slicker. He was a foreigner from Cyrene, a region in Libya (Acts 2:10) of North Africa. In fact, this particular region of West and North Africa is where Africans, were captured like wild animals, labeled as black gold on the market, transported like sardines over bodies of waters into a strange land. And at the same time beaten to death to learn our country's custom.

Africans as slaves, twenty of them landed in Virginia in 1619 during a storm. In 1641, slavery was legalized as a white collared occupation. In 1862, they experienced the Emancipation Proclamation. The Emancipation **Proclamation,** was Abraham Lincoln's declaration, that all slaves in all states which had seceded from the Union, and which had not returned to Federal control by 1863 January 1, would be emancipated.

In the text Simon of Cyrene was not a slave, but Simon was a man of color, who was forced to carry the cross of Jesus. Although he was not able to opt out; he discovered that the real pilgrimage was not at Jerusalem, but Golgotha. And at Golgotha is where many would be emancipated of their sins. It was a single act, and not a yearly Passover affair, and the sacrifice was the Precious Lamb of God. This pilgrimage is for everybody.

Oddly, the identity of Simon the Cyrene is as curious as his appearance before Jesus that day. He was faceless, nameless, and harmless in the crowd, but now he was singled out to be Jesus' pallbearer. During the days of the segregation; African Americans faced this same type of situation. They were faceless, nameless, harmless, and ultimately singled out.

While most theologians seldom question the color of his skin, there's many painting of Simon the Cyrene depicting him to be a black man! According to scripture they forced Simon the Cyrene to carry the cross. The black man symbolic acknowledgement of Jesus has always been the cross. The cross is what separates Christianity from other religions; the suffering Messiah from popular gurus, and the men of faith from the boys.

Throughout history there were many blacks; who carried the cross and help pave the way for the African Americans National Heritage. But, there's still work to be done before the dream of Dr. Martin Luther King Jr. in which people are judged by the content of their character instead of the color their skin is realized.

There are many outstanding achievers of all times, despite the color of their skin. Today we know about the achievements of Barack Obama, Condoleezza Rice, Nina Mitchell Wells, Oprah Winfrey, Bill Cosby, Denzel Washington, Ben Carson, Ted Wells, Tiger Woods, and Dick Parsons.

Their accomplishments are manifestations of African American History. Their contributions are a double edged sword. On the one hand they help eradicate the negative bias about the perceived inferiority of African Americans and provide sources of inspiration for others to emulate. On the other hand, the brilliance of their contributions can lead to the misconception that there is no longer any need for celebrating African American History. That is not true as a great number of African Americans are plagued by the aforementioned gaps which prevent them from participating fully in the pursuit of happiness.

Simon of Cyrene experienced this pursuit of happiness; when he carried the cross. There were many disciples named Simon, but where was Simon Peter, the leader of the twelve apostles? Why did he not say something? Where was Simon the zealot when the Roman soldiers were crucifying the Lord? What happened to his anti-Roman zeal? Where was Simon, Jesus' half-brother, when their mother Mary was crying her tears out (Mk 6:3)?

Jesus has to rely upon a black man to help Him bear the cross. The shame of the cross to the Greeks, Jews, and to the world was understandable. We need big bodies, broad shoulders, and brave hearts for the journey. Simon the frequent traveler was right for the job. In the end, Simon became Jesus side show, the butt of jokes and object of ridicule.

Whether Simon knew it, meant it, or treasured it, he was still serving Jesus. The walk behind Jesus was unanticipated. If he walked in front of Jesus he could have reached Golgotha easily in half the time. But to walk behind Jesus, you will have to slow down every time Jesus slowed, paused, or tripped. You cannot walk fast, be frantic, or arrive first. Simon saw Jesus fall three times. He heard Jesus breathe a sigh of relief, and then struggled for air, but eventually reached Golgotha. Charles Haddon Spurgeon said, "There are no crown-wearers in heaven who were not cross—bearers here below."

If you do not carry the cross on earth, you do not have a crown in heaven. Some of us had to be pushed by force, others pulled by the love of God, but push or pull, you will carry the cross in your lifetime. And God desires you and me to be strong enough to carry the cross, slow enough to follow Him, and spirited enough to finish the course. Like Simon, you will discover the strength to bear the cross, the shame, and the load. And when you embrace the cross, endure the shame; you will exchange it for a crown. Today, the pilgrimage is not a pilgrimage to Jerusalem, Mecca or Golgotha once in your lifetime, nor to Jerusalem every year at the Passover, but the true biblical pilgrimage is to deny yourself, take up the cross daily and follow Jesus (Luke 9:23).

Chapter 23

⌒⌒

I Need You to Survive

(2 Timothy 3:1-5 KJV)
*This know also, that in the last days perilous times
shall come. For men shall be lovers of their own selves,
covetous, boasters, proud, blasphemers, disobedient to
parents, unthankful, unholy, Without natural affection,
trucebreakers, false accusers, incontinent, fierce, despisers
of those that are good, Traitors, heady, highminded,
lovers of pleasures more than lovers of God; Having a
form of godliness, but denying the power thereof: from
such turn away.*

These are days when Christians are being pressed upon, and attacked from every angle. Thank God He has left us with the Holy Scriptures, a guidebook for survival. God is so concerned about our humanistic direction; he decided to incorporate us with His Rhema Word (the spoken word), in a biblical expression of His Deity. This was exclusively, spoken by the ancient Prophets, as the spirit gave them utterance. Look at the tenor and tone of the Word presented to us as our spiritual geographical road map to heaven. The Bible!

BIBLE STATISTICS:
B-Basic I-Instructions B-Before L-Leaving E-Earth

Old Testament	New Testament
1. 39 books	27 books
2. 929 chapters	260 chapters
3. 23,214 verses	7959 verses
4. 593,493 words	181,253 word
5. Longest book Psalms	Longest—Act
6. Shortest book Obadiah	Shortest—3 John
7. 17 Historical books	4 Gospel
8. 5 Poetical books	1 Historical book
9. 17 Prophetical books	22 Epistles

I. Affirmed Accountability:

Here in the text we are reading the General Pastoral Epistle of inspired ministerial advice from Paul to Timothy. He was instructing Timothy on how to guide and rule the Lord's church. It won't be long until Paul is beheaded under the guillotine of Nero's chopping block. So he leaves Timothy with words of comfort that it will get worse before it gets better.

We are warned in 2 Timothy's presentational revelation, that "**perilous times will come**" (2 Timothy 3:1). The word *perilous* is interesting. Its meaning spiritually is conducive to one with a terminal illness. Subjectively it references: exceedingly fierce times, dangerous times, frightening times, hazardous times, terrible times that must be greatly avoided! Or one will suffer detrimental consequences.

In fact, It's used only twice in the Bible, here and in Matthew 8:28, where two men who were demon possessed are referenced as "exceedingly fierce."

The writer preferably Paul, hits the target bull's-eye by explaining descriptively, that exceedingly fierce days shall come. Our world is facing moral crisis, spiritual crisis, social crisis, political crisis, and economic crisis. We look around and see nations collapsing, and a universe in sinful delusional disarray. The Bible tells us about all of these things. Look at 2 Timothy 3:2-7 to see what the last days are going to be like.

People will live for self alone in these peculiar days:

This philosophy has been put rather graphically in a jingle that says,

> **I had a little tea party**
> **this afternoon at three.**
> **Twas very small, three guests in all,**
> **just I, myself and me.**
>
> **Myself ate up the sandwiches,**
> **and I drank up the tea.**
> **Twas also I who ate the pie,**
> **and passed the cake to me.**

There are eighteen ways many people live a self-centered life listed in these few verses:

II. Identify the Inadvisable:

They will be **lovers of themselves**; and exist for what they can grab not what they can give. They will be **covetous** which means "lovers of money and possessions." They will **boast** about their great civilization and not about our creator, **proudly** exalting themselves. They will be **blasphemers** instead of blessing others. The children will be **disobedient** to their parents. They will be **unthankful** with no sense of gratitude or appreciation, for what God or others have done for them past, present and future.

They will be, **unholy** maintaining the outward form of religion, but they will deny its power. They will be **without natural affection**, arrogant, and lovers of insult. There will be **trucebreakers**; breakers of promises and agreements. There will be **false accusers** of the innocent. They will be **incontinent**; undisciplined with no self control. This person refuses to get professional help!

They desire more drinks, sex, pornography, drugs, and smoking to satisfy their passion. They will be **fierce**; instead of murdering they mutilate, torture and kill at random. There will be **despisers of those who are good**, targeting those who refuse to speak up for themselves. There will be **traitors**, one who will turn on his best friend. They will be **heady**, one who thinks they know it all. They will be **highminded**, one who's conceited and think he's above everyone else. There will be **lovers of pleasures** more than lovers of God. They will have a form of godliness, but denying the powers thereof. Paul warns Timothy, that people of these sorts to avoid (2 Tim. 3:2-5).

Don't let this discourage you. Though things may seem to be out of control in your life right now! I need you to survive. To God your life is not out of control. It's just right! As a matter of fact, this passage shows us that God is in complete control. None of these things have escaped His notice. He has foretold these last days. They are a precursor to the return of Jesus Christ.

When these things begin to happen, the Bible says, "Don't look around. Don't look down. Look up and lift up your heads, because your deliverance draws near" (Luke 21:28).

There are also some keys to surviving perilous days found in 2 Timothy. God has shown us specifically what to do. We're to turn away from people whose lives are inundated with the ways of the world (2 Timothy 3:5). This doesn't mean to recoil from the lost with whom we want to share Christ's love. We must separate ourselves from those who profess Christianity, yet live a double standard life. In some area of our lives we are a guilty of living a life of double standards.

You cannot fellowship with someone who willfully pursues impure and immoral things and acts as if nothing is wrong with it. You ought to treat people who are embracing a life of ungodliness as you would treat those who have a dangerous disease. Be careful you might catch something dangerous and viral! Select your friends according to the Scriptures.

III. Prepare for Persecution:

You should also **Prepare for Persecution,** if you desire to live godly in these last days (v. 12). The word *persecution* comes from a root word which means "to pursue." It means people are going to inspect you, seeking to find slipups with you, so they can call you out and disapprove of you. You may think that if you live a godly life, you'll escape persecution. But, it's just the opposite. So, prepare to bare ridicule as a badge of honor when you take a stand for what is right. The Lord will be near and precious to you when you are laughed at and mocked for your loyalty. Trust that He will see you through.

IV. Study the Scriptures:

Lastly, **Study the Scriptures** because the world is not getting any better. It's only going to get worse (v. 13), and the Word of God is going to be your assurance. It will help you endure the battle set before us (v. 14). Knowing the Scriptures will help you win people to Christ (v. 15). And it will equip you with Truth and Righteousness, so you are not unarmed in these evil times (vs. 16, 17). You need to be saturated with the Word of God and motivated by the Spirit of God so you can be activated in the battle.

God is a blesser, not a blaster. He wants the best for us. He gave his Son Christ Jesus for us. We enjoy the abundant blessings of a loving Heavenly Father. Yet there is an aspect to the Christian life that includes suffering. Rather than be thrown off guard by hardship and suffering, let us rather look upon it as an opportunity to grow in our Christian experience.

Chapter 24

⟡

A Great Tsunami is on the Way

(Matthew 24:36-41 KJV)
But of that day and hour knoweth no man, no, not the angels of heaven, but my Father only. But as the days of Noah were, so shall also the coming of the Son of man be. For as in the days that were before the flood they were eating and drinking, marrying and giving in marriage, until the day that Noe entered into the ark, And knew not until the flood came, and took them all away; so shall also the coming of the Son of man be. Then shall two be in the field; the one shall be taken, and the other left. Two women shall be grinding at the mill; the one shall be taken, and the other left.

I heard a story of a young preacher who had just begun his sermon on the second coming of Christ. He was a little uneasy, and about ten minutes into the message his mind went blank. He remembered what they had taught him in seminary; when a situation like this would arise. The professor informed him to take his time and repeat his last point. Often this would help you remember what was coming next. So he thought he would give it a try. "Behold, I come quickly," he said. Still his mind was blank. He thought he would try it again. "Behold I come quickly." Still nothing happened. He tried it one more time with such force that he fell forward, knocking the pulpit to one side, tripping over a flowerpot, and falling into the lap of a little old lady in the front row. The young preacher apologized and tried to explain what happened. "That's all right, young man," said the little old lady. "It was my fault. I should have gotten out of the way. After you told me three times you were coming!" Although we may be warned of impending danger, we often do not heed the warning.

We are roughly in the middle of what is known as the Olivet discourse where Jesus is teaching from the Mount of Olives (Matthew 24-25). We are entering into a zone where there is a diversity of opinion as to how to understand what Jesus says. We are looking at Matthew 24: 36-41, where Jesus is speaking about the coming of the Son of Man. (Matthew 24:36) is speaking about the return of Jesus that clearly says, *"But of that day and hour knoweth no man, no, not the angels of heaven, but my Father only."* How much clearer can the Bible make it than that!

When will Jesus come back? The angels in heaven don't know. Jesus doesn't know Himself. Only God the Father knows. Please hear these words from Matthew's gospel. Its truth is authentic. You can turn on the television right now and probably hear some televangelist talking about Jesus coming back soon. But if you simply read what it says in the Bible, it says that Jesus doesn't even know when his return will be! So, either those who preach about such things are smarter than Jesus, or they are misguided and they are misguiding others.

Despite this clear, black and white statement of His claim. People still continue to examine the details of prophecy to calculate when Jesus will return. It is like well, maybe we cannot know the day or hour but maybe the week or month or year! Matthew 24:36, is very clear "no one knows" means know one can. Not the angels, not even Jesus himself. But this knowledge is only known by God the Father, who's omniscient.

I. The Speculation of His Return:

In the course of centuries gone by, there have been two hundred predictions concerning Christ return. There was a prediction reported as, May 21, 2011 as—Judgment Day; October 21, 2011—as the end of the world. These date setters all have one thing in common; they are all wrong! If Christ had wanted us to know the date of His return, He would have told us clearly, somewhere in the 66 books of the bible.

Biblical prophecy and eschatology are both fascinating, and spiritually encouraging subjects, as any Christian who has studied them will testify. They are also difficult subjects to deal with responsibly because not all prophecy is equally clear.

But if the Bible is clear on anything, it is that no one knows the specific time of Christ's return. Thus, when Christ said that no one knows the time of His return, He obviously included present-day believers. "So you also must be ready, because the Son of Man will come at an hour when you do not expect Him" (Matthew 24:44). Don't get caught slipping; for some reason, a lot of Christians aren't listening to Jesus.

Jesus will come like a tsunami, but quicker! A tsunami is described as a series of catastrophic ocean waves generated by submarine movements, which may be caused by volcanic eruptions, landslides beneath the ocean, or an asteroid striking the earth. Tsunamis are also called seismic sea waves or, popularly, tidal waves. In the open ocean, tsunamis may have wavelengths of up to several hundred miles and travel at speeds up to 500 miles per hour, yet have wave heights of less than 3 feet, destroying everything in its path; like that great tsunami which struck Japan.

This is the warning that we receive from Jesus Christ today. In our scripture, Jesus reminds us over and over again that his return will be the same as a thief that comes in the night to break in, steal, and destroy. He warns us that when he comes again, many people will be living their lives the same as usual, and that many will not be watching. The same is true with death, as well. People by and large continue with their daily lives right up to the point of passing from this earth.

Interestingly, many businesses and industries use the phrase "An Equal Opportunity Employer" to show that they will accept anyone, regardless of race, nationality, religion, and even sexual preference. Such is the case with death. Death comes to everyone, in every walk of life, at every age, and in every country in the world. Death is, "An Equal Opportunity Employer." Death took the David's young child, old man Methuselah, rich man Nebuchadnezzar, poor man Lazarus, untrustworthy Zacchaeus, wise man Solomon, and the foolish man Balaam. Death took devious Delia, crossed eyed Leah, painted face Jezebel, praying Hanna, romantic Ruth, two faced Miriam, sentimental Mary Magdalene, and crying Mary the mother of Jesus. Death comes to everyone, and will continue to come to people, should the Lord Jesus continue to tarry on his second coming.

Time is winding up! How do you know? Balance is unstable, bones are fable, mind playing tricks on you, skin is wrinkling, teeth are collapsing, eyes are losing focus, sounds of the world has arrested your eardrums, taste bugs are marching away, knees won't bend nor will they bow, blood count low; sometime to high, sugar count isn't good enough, heart won't beat right, kidneys won't functions, liver won't filter, and were living in a world that's gone wild. But don't you worry, still praise Him! "A Great Tsunami is on the Way!"

The question is, are you ready to meet God? If today is your day, or if Jesus Christ should return with the shout and the trumpet, would you be ready to stand in front of God for the judgment?

II. The Simplification of His Return:

The simplification of His return is the preaching of His word. Jesus is coming! Stop swimming around in immorality that will get you left behind. Question! Why did Jesus mention, Noah's day in the scripture? It took Noah quite a long time to build the ark; a lot of planning, a lot of hard work, and a lot of mockery. In contrast to his preaching, and the length of time it took; the flood when it intruded their territory was swift, and it was sudden. Jesus doesn't emphasise the sinfulness of the people in Noah's time instead he emphasises something else to make his point.

The people during the time of Noah were simply living life. Life was merely rolling along as it usually did. Jesus makes it clear about his return, that it will be a day just like any other day. Back then, you would have been able to see Noah building the ark. And back then you would have heard as to why. But as life went on no one cared. Life just rolled on until it was too late.

But as the days of Noah were, so shall also the coming of the Son of man be. For as in the days that were before the flood they were eating and drinking, marrying and giving in marriage, until the day that Noe entered into the ark, And knew not until the flood came, and took them all away; so shall also the coming of the Son of man be (Matthew 24:37-39).

In Noah's time unbelievers were judged and condemned: Notice what Jesus says in verse 37, *"But as the days of Noah were, so shall also the coming of the Son of man be."* Now what happened in the days of Noah? God saved Noah and his family, who were righteous, and then God judged the rest of the world with a flood. The flood is the only event in human history that comes close to illustrating what will happen in the end times.

We read in verse 39 that the flood "took them all away." They were swept away with a flood of judgment. Then Jesus said in the last of verse 39, "so also will the coming of the Son of Man be."

The Judgment of the Second Coming will not be a flood of water, but with fire and brimstone next time. Remember, Noah was "a preacher of righteousness" (2 Peter 2:5). Yet in spite of his preaching in both word and deed, they were unconcerned. They simply ignored Noah and continued to live "as always," eating and drinking, marrying and giving in marriage (verse 38).

They failed to realize their perilous situation until it was too late. I can just picture many people banging on the door of the ark, asking to be saved from the rising flood. Similarly, people during the end times will notice all the signs and wonders going on around them, but many of them won't consider what's happening and why. Many people will not believe what they hear until it's too late.

You better make sure that you have truly repented of your sins and that you have received the Lord Jesus as your personal Savior. Don't imagine that you have plenty of time to be saved. As someone once said, "Eternity is too long to be wrong." God's Word to the unsaved is, "Be ready."

III. The Separation of His Return:

In that great day, when Christ comes again, there will be a great separation:

The godly and the ungodly, the righteous and the wicked, the elect and the reprobate are mingled together in this world. In the church, in the factory, in the field, and in the family the children of God and the children of the devil are side by side. But it shall not always be so. When Christ comes again, there shall be a great separation made. In a moment, in the twinkling of an eye, at last trumpet's sound, these two groups shall be forever separated. In that great and terrible day, the divisions and separation of the godly from the ungodly will be decisive, immediate, and everlasting.

- Husbands from wives;
- Mothers from children;
- Brothers from sisters;
- Pastors from hearers;
- Friends from friends.

There will be no time for repentance. There will be opportunities for grace. As you are in that day, so you shall be forever! Believers shall be caught up to heaven, glory, honor, and eternal life. Unbelievers shall be snatched away and cast into hell, damnation, and eternal destruction and death. Let us therefore make our calling and election sure, both by faith and by works of righteousness, which are the inevitable fruit of true faith.

Chapter 25

⌒⁓⁓

Encourage Yourself

(1 Samuel 30:6 KJV)
*And David was greatly distressed; for the people spake
of stoning him, because the soul of all the people was
grieved, every man for his sons and for his daughters: but
David encouraged himself in the LORD his God.*

In the onset of this text, David and his men had gone to help king Achish in battle. When they returned to Ziglag they found the city burned and families gone. David's men turned on him and spoke of stoning him because of this invasion. The Amalekites once nomadic people of Canaan said in the Bible to be descendants of Esau's grandson Amalek were responsible for this mischievous deed.

In my researching I discovered that Ziglag was given by King Achish of Gath to David when he was running from Saul, and David used Ziglag for a home base for raids against various groups who threatened the southern borders of Judah (1 Samuel 27).

I. The Misery of David's Life:

It was David's darkest hour. It was an hour of crisis, trial and disaster. Here is a scene of devastation and destruction. The people they loved the most were now taken away from them, and taken captive by the Amalekites, and their homes have been burnt to the ground. Instead of coming together as one, the men David depended on the most turned against him seeking to stone him. Look at David while he bathes in his darkest hours of despair. Not David! He was a man after God's own heart (1 Samuel 13:14).

He's in a time of:

- Distress—This was an Acute physical discomfort for David;
- Despair—He must have felt a sense of futility or defeat;
- Disappointment—all that he had accomplished has now become a defeated achievement.

While they had been out to battle, their enemies, the Amalekites, had raided, and looted, and captured the women, their mothers, their sisters, their wives, their children, and had taken them as slaves. Here's David the one who would become king within 72 hours, who would wear the finest robes now left with just the clothes he wore on his back, because everything he owned had been deliberately taken away from him! Carried off by the raiders; his home was a mass of smoldering embers.

David's men were devastated and distressed by this great tragedy:

Then David and the people that were with him lifted up their voice and wept, until they had no more power to weep (Verse 4).

Some sat down and wept till they had no more tears to shed. Some complained and blamed David. But David stared disaster in the face with the eyes of faith to overcome the temporary accomplishment of the enemy. What do you do when life falls apart?

II. The Magnification of David's Life:

Although this situation seemed to agitate, and aggravated David and his men, one thing that the Amalekites could not agitate and aggravate is David's relationship with God. David turned to the Lord for strength to face these critical circumstances. They could not rob David's relationship with God.

Although David could no longer say, **"My house, my city, my possessions**," he could say, "My God." All of us should be infected with a **"My God Praise**." Let everything that has breath praise the Lord!

David encouraged himself in the Lord. He was greatly distressed, but David encouraged himself in the Lord his God. When you face desperate times, and face great trouble, you can still gain encouragement in the Lord. Encouraging yourself in the Lord means you remind yourself about what the Word says about God and His promises and apply those truths to your current situation.

David asked of the Lord:

And David inquired of the LORD, "Shall I pursue after thisband? Shall I overtake them?" He answered him, "Pursue, for you shall surely overtake and shall surely rescue" (Verse 8).

He sought counsel from God. At this dark hour, after years of a hard life, running from Saul and battling the enemies of Israel. He went to the Lord in prayer. We all have those times when we feel at the end of our own strength, when we face pain or disappointments. David had one person who was closer than a brother that he knew he could lean upon. Even while some folk were looking to pick which stones to execute him! Even though David himself was grieving because of the capture of his two wives! Even though David was distressed! The Word says *"David Encouraged himself in the LORD his GOD."*

David got the victory there, by faith. He was encouraging himself in the presence of the Lord. He was rejoicing in God's faithfulness and he came to see that all that really counts in the face of death and despair is a personal knowledge of God. Listen! God wants you to take His promises and run with them. As you drive through life, use the windshield and not the rearview mirror. Don't look back; keep the Faith and look up!

III. The Manifestation of David's Life:

Remember God will bring about a change! I once heard a story concerning a little boy who was trying to encourage himself by saying, "I'm the best batter in the world!" and then tossing a ball into the air and swinging at it. He missed three times, though. So he then said, "I'm the best pitcher in the world!" So when the bottom falls out, do not give up. Renew your heart with God and press in close to Him. David did just that!

How tempted David must have been to quit! Instead, he encouraged himself in the Lord. He rallied the troops and went out after the enemy! In the darkest moment of his life, he was just hours away from the fulfillment of God's Promise! David got back his fight and immediately acted in faith. The Lord heard David, and He will hear you also! When you cry out from a horrible pit, He hears. You may be in the furnace, but you'll come out without the smell of smoke. You may be in the lion's den, but God has sent an angel to lock their jaws.

All that David and his men lost, all that David and his men recovered:

And David recovered all that the Amalekites had carried away: and David rescued his two wives. And there was nothing lacking to them, neither small nor great, neither sons nor daughters, neither spoil, nor any thing that they had taken to them: David recovered all (Verse 18-19).

Contact Information:

Dr. Richie Bell, Jr.
Pilgrim Travelers' Missionary Baptist Church
604 Harrison Street
Shreveport, Louisiana 71106
(318) 688-8045
bpsermon@bellsouth.net

For more information:
Visit us @ www.blackpreachersermon.com